CANDIDE

Borgo Press Books by CLÉMENT VAUTEL & LÉO MARCHÈS

Candide

Borgo Press Books by VOLTAIRE

The Death of Caesar
Oedipus
Saul and David
Socrates

CANDIDE

A PLAY IN FIVE ACTS

CLÉMENT VAUTEL &

LÉO MARCHÈS

Translated and Adapted by Frank J. Morlock
From the Novel by Voltaire

THE BORGO PRESS
MMXIII

CANDIDE

Copyright © 2000, 2013 by Frank J. Morlock

FIRST BORGO PRESS EDITION

Published by Wildside Press LLC

www.wildsidebooks.com

DEDICATION

For my dear friend, Doctor Ernesto Ibarra

CONTENTS

CAST OF CHARACTERS 9
ACT I, Scene 1 13
ACT I, Scene 2 33
ACT II, Scene 3 49
ACT II, Scene 4 65
ACT III, Scene 5 81
ACT IV, Scene 6 105
ACT IV, Scene 7 129
ACT V, Scene 8 159
ACT V, Scene 9 169
ABOUT THE AUTHOR 183

CAST OF CHARACTERS

CANDIDE

PANGLOSS

CACAMBO

MARTIN

DON FERNANDO

GOOD OLD TURK

BARON

KING OF THE BULGARS

The GRAND INQUISITOR

2nd MONARCH

4th MONARCH

JESUIT

DON ISSACHAR

1st MONARCH

ECCLESIASTIC

3rd MONARCH

GRAND ALMONER

DECEIVED HUSBAND

1st NCO

ALGUAZIL

2nd NCO

WORKER

PACIFIST

1st PIKEMAN

2nd PIKEMAN

YOUNG MAN

LACKEY

2nd YOUNG MAN

OFFICER OF ST. HERMANDAD

SECRETARY

INHABITANT OF LISBON

CUNEGONDE

OLD WOMAN

BARONESS

OPULENT MAIDEN

PAQUETTE

YOUNG WOMAN

BEAUTIFUL GIRL

1st FEMALE INHABITANT

2nd FEMALE INHABITANT

SERVANT

WOMAN

ACT I
SCENE 1

In the back a dilapidated Château, but possessing a door and windows. In front of the Château a small forest, baptized a park. Thickets and wild flowers—

BARON

(Entering) Hey! My pikeman! My wife! My Grand Almoner! Hey! Candide! Cunegonde! Hey Pangloss! Hey! Everybody—! I am very dissatisfied—I am furious—!

(Enter the Baroness followed by the Grand Almoner)

BARONESS

What's the matter with you, my friend?

BARON

The matter is, Baroness—That I intend to remain master here—Am I no longer the high and mighty Baron Thunder-ten-Tronchk?

BARONESS

You still are my friend!

GRAND ALMONER

One of the most respected lords of Westphalia, whose Grand Almoner I have the honor to be—when I am not watching over the health of the souls of the Parish in my capacity as vicar.

BARON

(Going back and forth waving his whip) Where are my people? I think I haven't yet whipped them today!

GRAND ALMONER

Milord, you treat them with too much kindness—that type mustn't be treated too kindly.

BARON

Yes, I am too good. (Enter two pikemen). Ah—! There you are—swine, brigands—scoundrels—

GRAND ALMONER

Ask Milord's pardon—

1st PIKEMAN

What did we do? (The Baron runs after them and administers his whip to them)

GRAND ALMONER

Don't run away like that—You'll tire the Baron.

BARON

(To Pikeman) I ought to hang you from the postern gate of my castle—You want to kill my honorable dogs, the most beautiful dogs of Westphalia—dogs of pedigree—noble dogs?

1st PIKEMAN

By doing what, Milord?

BARON

By feeding them the way you do—wretches! You gorge them.

1st PIKEMAN

Once a day I give them bread dipped in dishwater—and sometimes some bones left by Milord and his illustrious family—

BARON

That's too much! My dogs are dying of indigestion—just as you will die yourselves—ruffians—Here the whole world eats too much—beasts and people.

BARONESS

It's true. They've been gorged!

GRAND ALMONER

They are being delivered to the sin of gourmandizing.

BARON

It's a scandal! I intend that this stop, you understand? (Brandishing his whip) My house is not an inn where everyone can stuff themselves at my expense to that extent! The animals and the people in my service have appetites that don't coincide with their social position. Small folks must have small stomachs.

BARONESS

That's evident!

GRAND ALMONER

That's fair.

BARON

I will see to that. Besides, I am very dissatisfied with the appearance and the administration of my Château—

GRAND ALMONER

Which is one of the most beautiful castles in Westphalia!

BARON

An evil spirit reigns. The servants are inclined more and more to deviate from the good traditions of the past— Not only that, they eat too much but they permit themselves to argue. It's unheard of! And when employing the rights my birth conferred upon me. I wish to correct them by switching their backsides with the whip God confided in me—They dare to take flight—!

PIKEMAN

Pardon us, Milord.

GRAND ALMONER

You will accuse yourselves of great sins when you come to confess—

BARON

Submission—respect—are gone—I ask myself what we are coming to—Poor Westphalia—you are heading toward the abyss! Happily—I am here—

GRAND ALMONER

We are here—!

BARON

I am going to put an end to this state of things so that my Château, which is the most beautiful castle in Westphalia will regain its fine appearance—! Two ways to do that! First of all, my whip! And then moral education—good, clean ideas—

GRAND ALMONER

I will answer for that—

BARON

No, my Grand Almoner, I have appointed you to my personal service as well as that of the Baroness. I have here a professor of Philosophy that I pay to instruct my daughter Miss Cunegonde and Candide, my nephew in the art of thinking.

BARONESS

Oh—your nephew—!

BARON

It is indeed true that my honorable sister who engendered him was not married. The gentleman who made this child was unable, you know, to justify more than seventy-one quarters when she possessed seventy-two. That's why my worthy sister finally refused him her hand, after having, alas accorded him the rest. But little matter—Dr. Pangloss, professor of Philosophy to my daughter and my nephew will also instruct my men—

BARONESS

Now that's an excellent thing, my friend.

BARON

The people need Philosophy. (He snaps his whip)

PIKEMAN

Long live the Baron! (Enter Paquette)

BARONESS

You hear, Paquette. Every day lessons from Doctor Pangloss.

PAQUETTE

(Laughing) He's an excellent professor—He's already taught me many curious things—(Enter Pangloss,

Cunegonde, and Candide)

PANGLOSS

I heard "Long Live the Baron," and I ran with my pupils to associate myself with this touching manifestation. "Long live the most powerful lord in Westphalia!"

BARON

Dr. Pangloss, I was waiting for you—I've decided to confide an important mission to you—a social one—! Here it is: I charge you with instructing my folks in the principles of goodness, of healthy philosophy—That which fortifies the role of masters and which affirms in the hearts of servants feelings of respect and submission—lastly—the philosophy which assures the happiness of individuals and social peace. Each day, at this hour, you will spread the good word.

PANGLOSS

I am very flattered—

BARON

You are going to begin immediately.

PANGLOSS

I am ready. A philosopher is always ready—I will instruct Milord's people in the most reasonable, the best of doctrines, that is to say—the metaphysical—theological, cosmological—pedagogical—

1ˢᵗ PIKEMAN

(To second) What'd he say?

2ⁿᵈ PIKEMAN

He was talking about pederast—

BARON

Silence! (Brandishes his whip)

CUNEGONDE

(To Baron) Papa, do I have to listen? I've taken my lesson.

CANDIDE

Me, too—

BARON

Both of you stay, as I myself am doing. The metaphysical—theological—cosmological (Stammering) Anyway, this pederasty is the most excellent thing in the world—You can't get too much of it. (To Pangloss) Begin, my friend!

CANDIDE

(To Cunegonde) It's all the same to me—better, since I am near you.

PANGLOSS

(After wiping his nose and grimacing) Milord Baron, Milady, Miss Cunegonde, Mr. Candide—Your reverence, the Grand Almoner, (Making bows) Paquette.

(With a slight gesture) You others—Like the great systems The Physical—Theological—Cosmological pedagogy clings to a very simple principle. That principle is this: There is no effect without a cause—That principle admitted it follows naturally that everything is for the best in the best of all possible worlds.

PIKEMAN

That depends—I've just been stung by a wasp.

BARON

Silence! (He brandishes his whip)

PANGLOSS

Note carefully that the nose was made for glasses—Also, we have glasses—The legs are visibly designed to be in stockings and we have stockings. Stones have been formed to be quarried for use in making castles.

That's why Milord Baron has a Château and pigs were made to be eaten—so we eat pork all year round. Whips were made to be wielded by great lords, so Milord the Baron has a whip—Servants have spines and that's why it's just they wait when their master wants to whip them. Everything is linked together, everything is in a chain—all is admirably organized in nature and consequently in society—Which is part of nature. To argue, to dispute, to protest.

BARON

To eat too much.

PANGLOSS

That demonstrates one is unworthy of embracing—

CANDIDE

(To Cunegonde) Who are they?

PANGLOSS

(Hurrying his speech) The Metaphysical—Theological Cosmological Pedagogy—which proves that this Château is the most beautiful of all possible Châteaux, that Milord Baron is the most generous, the most brave, the most powerful of all possible barons, that Milady the Baroness is the best possible Baroness—that the happy subjects who are at their service are the most happy of all possible subjects, and that the society in which we live is the most beautiful, the most just, the most admirable of all possible societies. (He wipes himself off)

BARON

Very fine! (To Pikemen) You understood—imbeciles?

PIKEMEN

(After a short hesitation) Long live the Baron!

PANGLOSS

You see they are perfectly convinced.

BARON

That suffices—Tomorrow, same thing—! Second lesson—Come Madame. Let's go into our beautiful castle. (He leaves followed by the Baroness and the Grand Almoner)

PANGLOSS

(To Pikemen) Go—Meditate on my instructions.

1st PIKEMAN

Us? You're joking—

PANGLOSS

What!—You dare? Just now in front of the Baron—

1st PIKEMAN

That's not the same thing. The Baron has a whip. (The Pikemen leave)

PANGLOSS

(To Candide and Cunegonde) Go take a stroll in the park. (They go) (To Paquette) You—Stay!

PAQUETTE

Ah, Mr. Pangloss, how well you talk! I didn't understand much, but—

PANGLOSS

It's really very simple—not only is everything good—but everything is for the best. So—here we are alone. Isn't that what we wish?

PAQUETTE

Fie, sir—you are a strange philosopher—And your theories.

PANGLOSS

(Squeezing her) Let's leave our theories.

PAQUETTE

Your speech—

PANGLOSS

It's really a question of speeches—(Grabs her by the waist and embraces her) No words, deeds!

PAQUETTE

(Not resisting) What kind of Philosophy is that?

PANGLOSS

Always the same. There's no effect without a cause. You have the prettiest possible figure—it's made to be taken—And I am taking it—You have the rosiest, the freshest mouth possible—it was made to be kissed and I am kissing it.

PAQUETTE

Oh—but someone could see us.

PANGLOSS

Come, delicious Paquette—match your arguments

against mine in this ditch. It will be very well for us to see if the same causes always produce the same effects. (He leads her into the ditch at the same time as Candide and Cunegonde enter the same ditch)

CANDIDE

Let's continue to inform ourselves, darling Cunegonde.

CUNEGONDE

Without a doubt it's a lesson in Philosophy—a private lesson! (They observe the frolics of Pangloss and Paquette which have become invisible)

CANDIDE

That to me has the appearance of experimental physics.

CUNEGONDE

Paquette appears to me to be very advanced—

CANDIDE

Yes—She's a fine pupil.

CUNEGONDE

Experimental physics is a very interesting science.

CANDIDE

Thrilling!

CUNEGONDE

Ah, Candide, it seems to me, that I too, I have an inclination towards this beautiful science.

CANDIDE

My darling Cunegonde.

CUNEGONDE

My dear Candide—I feel very—moved—

CANDIDE

I have a heart that beats—that beats—(Cunegonde lets her fan fall—Candide picks it up—He takes her hand gracefully—and kisses it with excitement. She smiles—He embraces her)

BARON

(First speechless, then raising his arm) Oh!

BARONESS

(Raising her arm) For goodness sakes!

GRAND ALMONER

(Raising his arm) Heavens!

CANDIDE

I won't do it anymore!

BARON

Bandit!

BARONESS

Swine!

GRAND ALMONER

Rake! (The Baron rushes at Candide, who flees—he catches him and gives him a big kick in the behind that propels him into the wings)

BARON

Don't let me ever see you here again—for any reason. (Meanwhile the Baroness has socked Cunegonde who promptly faints)

GRAND ALMONER

Oh! My God! What a tragedy in the beautiful Château of Milord and Milady—I implore the aid of Heaven!

(Enter Pangloss and Paquette, then the servants)

PANGLOSS

What's going on? (The Baron returns)

BARON

That dirty rat allowed himself to embrace my daughter—I've given him a big kick in the ass—!

PAQUETTE

(Aside) Poor boy!

PANGLOSS

Well—There's an excellent proof of my philosophy. Candide has an ass and Milord the Baron has a foot—! The foot is quite naturally lodged in that ass.—Which proves everything is made for the best end—and that everything is for the best in the best of all possible worlds.

CUNEGONDE

(Coming to) Oh, Mother, it was despite me that he embraced me—I swear it!

PANGLOSS

The honor of Miss Cunegonde is avenged. The Baron

is the most fair and most powerful lord in Westphalia. The Baroness is the most vigilant and worthy of mothers—Therefore my friends. Let's shout "Long live the Baron! Long live the Baroness!"

ALL

"Long live the Baron! Long live the Baroness!"

BLACKOUT

ACT I
SCENE 2

A public square called a Square of Arms in the Bulgarian village of Waldberghoff—Trark—Bdikdorff surrounded by Bulgarian style houses.

On the right, a cabaret, by the door of which are seated at a table, with bottles and two glasses, two NCO recruiters for the glorious Bulgarian Army.

AT RISE, the two NCOs are seated at the table—clinking their glasses.

1st NCO

I drink to the health of His Majesty, The King of the Bulgars, our glorious sovereign. (Rising) To the health of His Majesty, The King of the Bulgars—our glorious sovereign (They drink and sit back down. The 2nd NCO rises after having filled both cups) I drink to the glorious Bulgarian army. (They drink)

2nd NCO

(Rising and clinking his glass with his comrade) To the Glorious Bulgarian Army. (They drink, refill and without sitting) To the Glorious Bulgarian infantry! (They drink) To the Glorious Bulgarian Cavalry. (They drink, fill up, etc)

1st NCO

To the Glorious Bulgarian artillery!

2nd NCO

To the Glorious Bulgarian artillery! (They drink)

1st NCO

(Raising a bottle) The bottles are empty. And we still have to drink to the glorious Bulgarian genius, the glorious Bulgarian Quartermaster, and the glorious Bulgarian health service.

2nd NCO

That will be for tonight, tomorrow and the day after. We have plenty of time!

1st NCO

No—Tomorrow and the days following we will have to celebrate the glorious victories of the glorious

Bulgarian army.

2ⁿᵈ NCO

To which we contribute by sending to battle all the brave young men, healthy and well built, and measuring at least five feet four that we can recruit. (With a cordial glance to a handsome young man who passes by) Hey, there!—Handsome blonde fellow—A little glass of wine? (The person spoken to responds with negative disdain and makes off speedily)

1ˢᵗ NCO

That didn't work. Attention, have a peep at those strapping fellows! That's our business. (Two young vigorous men come forward, turning) Well, comrades, it's a great day—war has been declared!

2ⁿᵈ NCO

Let's all shout, "Long live war!"

THE TWO YOUNG MEN

(Weakly) Long live war!

2ⁿᵈ NCO

Bravo.

1st NCO

(Trying to pull them) Come, comrades, we are going to enroll you under the laughing banner.

1st YOUNG MAN

(Pulling away, sneering) Do you think so?

2nd YOUNG MAN

No—just a joke.

2nd NCO

But anyway—come shout, "Long live war!"

1st YOUNG MAN

I'll do that when you leave me in peace. (The two young men move away)

1st NCO

Another misfire! It's not going good. They're shouting but they are not marching. That's no good for the war! (Noticing Candide who comes in skinny and ragged) Here, I think, is game less able to defend itself. His plumage is dull and his stomach probably empty. Let's see.

2ⁿᵈ NCO

That's it—let's spring the trap. (The 1ˢᵗ NCO, followed by the 2ⁿᵈ NCO, advances towards Candide)

1ˢᵗ NCO

(To Candide with an engaging smile and a military salute) Greetings, comrade.

2ⁿᵈ NCO

Comrade, greetings!

CANDIDE

(Civilly removing his hat) Gentlemen, I am indeed your servant.

1ˢᵗ NCO

Nice time for a stroll, right comrade?

CANDIDE

(Drying his face) A little warm!

2ⁿᵈ NCO

A glass of wine wouldn't be scorned, right, comrade?

CANDIDE

(At once tempted and cautious) Oh, sir—

1ˢᵗ NCO

With a good slice of Westphalia ham?

CANDIDE

From Westphalia—Alas.

2ⁿᵈ NCO

Some well marinated, sour cabbage, a bowl of cheese curds—and pastries from Sophia—

CANDIDE

(More and more tempted) Alas! Beautiful dream.

1ˢᵗ NCO

By God, comrade—We'll do you justice.

2ⁿᵈ NCO

And you will dine with us!

CANDIDE

Gentlemen, you do me much honor but I don't have the wherewithal to pay mine.

1st NCO

Ah, sir—men with your look and your deserts—never pay!

2nd OFFICER

Aren't you at least five feet five inches high?

CANDIDE

You, sir, that's my height!

1st NCO

Ah, sir—sit yourself down. Not only we will pay for you, but won't ever suffer a man like you to lack money! Men are made to help each other.

CANDIDE

You are right. It's just like Dr. Pangloss my preceptor always told me, and I see—everything is for the best.

2nd NCO

(Passing him a pile of money) That's why you will please us by accepting these crowns with the effigy of our sovereign, the King of the Bulgars.

CANDIDE

Sir, you are indeed honest and I confess to you that such a present eases my circumstances and occurs very apropos—(He takes them) Please to accept all my thanks and allow me to recognize my debt to you by signing a promissory note—

1st NCO

What's that mean? No promissory notes between us— We are not money lenders, but good and brave soldiers. What's ours is yours, comrade—you will insult us by thinking otherwise.

CANDIDE

Gentlemen, gentlemen—I don't know how to recognize your bounty.

2nd NCO

You will thank us sir by doing us justice.—Let's go— to dine!

1st NCO

To dine—Hey—girls—Maritza, Nilchena, Petrovna— Serve us your best wine, your finest ham and your most distinguished provisions. (The servants leave the cabaret to hover around the three men, who've taken places at their table.

1st NCO (serving Candide)

Eat, young man!

CANDIDE

(Devouring the food) Gentlemen officers—I am confused and I didn't expect.

2nd NCO

(Pouring wine) Drink, young man.

1st NCO

And know, young foreigner, that Bulgarian hospitality is proverbial.

CANDIDE

(With his mouth full) I'm noticing—I would like to be able to thank you suitably.

2nd NCO

Don't thank us. What we are doing is quite natural.

1st NCO

Because we love you tenderly.

CANDIDE

(A bit surprised) Ah, really?

2nd NCO

And you, comrade, don't you love tenderly?

CANDIDE

Oh!—Yes—I love Miss Cunegonde tenderly—who is the most beautiful of women. But, Alas! I never see her anymore, for having embraced her, I was ignominiously kicked out of the Château of Thunder-ten-Tronckh—the most beautiful of castles—by my uncle, one of the most powerful lords of Westphalia.

1st NCO

That's quite possible—But it's not a question of Miss Cunegonde. We are asking you if you don't tenderly love the King of the Bulgars.

CANDIDE

Not at all, for I've never seen him.

2nd NCO

What! He's the most charming of Kings. You must drink to his health.

CANDIDE

Oh! Very willingly, gentlemen, since that is so agreeable to you. (Rising and lifting his glass) To the health of the King of the Bulgars. (Drinks)

1st NCO

(Rising) That's enough, you will support him, sustain him, defend him—The hero of the Bulgars—your fortune is made and your glory is assured.

CANDIDE

(Astonished) How can that be? Because I drank?

2nd NCO

Yes, young man! That toast has the value of a solemn oath. You are enrolled in the glorious Bulgarian army.

CANDIDE

Pardon, gentlemen, but I am Westphalian, and I have no intention of serving the King of the Bulgars. (The 1st NCO goes into the cabaret and emerges with a military cap which he places on Candide's head, a shoulder belt which he passes to him and a rifle which he wants Candide to hold between his arms) Ah, allow me, gentlemen. I protest.

2nd NCO

About what? Mutiny, already? You will catch it my boy. (Puts handcuffs on him)

1st NCO

Silence—and you've got to march right or failing that a flogging. (A military march is heard approaching. The Glorious Bulgarian army makes its entry to the acclamations of the crowd accompanying it. The two NCO's encircle Candide who struggling takes his place in the line.)

COMMANDER'S VOICE

Halt! Left face!

CROWD

Long live the army!

COMMANDER

Port arms! Present arms!

CROWD

Long live The King! (The imposing King makes his entry surrounded by a brilliant cortege of officers. Candide, petrified keeps quiet. The two NCO's remove his cuffs and make him present arms. The King receives the troops while the fanfare renews its brass bellowing.)

KING

Soldiers, I am pleased with you—! And with you, as well, pale civilians: know that a new dawn of glory is rising in the firmament of Bulgaria! My cousin, the traitorous felonious and scorned King of the Abares, under the false pretext that my glorious army has pillaged and ravaged his territory, dared to declare war on me. I am going to have need of all of you, my children—Yes, my children, for I am your father—of you, soldiers to make you kill gloriously—of you, civilians—to make you pay gloriously, also—tenfold taxes. We are going to make war—a fresh and joyous war. We will burn towns, we will violate women, we will kill children—And a new luster well spread over our immortal Bulgaria, which marches in the avant-garde of civilization, soldiers and you, citizens, I invite you to shout with me "Long live the war."

UNANIMOUS SHOUT

Long live war! (Soldiers and civilians appear to be greatly enthused only one bourgeois with a placid face in the first rank of the crowd remains mute. The King silently appraises this spectator)

KING

Who is that man who remains mute in the general joy? (All eyes focus on the abstainer) Let him be brought to me (Several soldiers rush on the placid civilian, seize him violently and bring him before the sovereign not without roughing him up a little) Why don't you join in the general enthusiasm? Why don't you shout "Long live war!" like the good Bulgarians surrounding you? Are you a bad Bulgarian? A traitor?

PACIFIST

Sire, I am not Bulgarian—I am Dutch. I love Bulgaria, but I also love peace.

KING

Enough! That impious word will be punished as it deserves. Let him be given 4,000 whacks with the baton and shot tomorrow morning. That will teach him to be Dutch and love peace!

CROWD

Bravo! Bravo! Long live the King! Long live war! Death to the traitor! (They lead the pacifist away and rough him up more. Candide thinks he can escape. Discreetly he puts down his rifle and as rapidly and furtively disappears by way of the garden. But the two NCO's notice his attempt to escape)

1st NCO

And the other one there who's cutting and running. (Runs after Candide)

2nd NCO

(Running to) Stop him! Stop him!

KING

What's happening?

VOICES

It's a deserter—a spy! (The NCOs bring back Candide very badly mauled by the crowd. They place handcuffs on him and irons on his legs)

1st NCO

Sire, this man who enlisted this morning in the glorious army station attempted to take flight. (Exclamations of indignation)

KING

To take flight at the moment when he's going to have the honor of fighting—perhaps, dying for Bulgaria—! Are you such a coward?

CANDIDE

Sire, I am very unfortunate and I have no wish to die even for Bulgaria.

KING

That's enough of that! I cannot take anymore. Put him with the other traitor and let him undergo the same treatment: 4,000 blows with the baton and tomorrow morning a dozen bullets in his hide I have spoken.

CROWD

Long live the King—Long live Bulgaria!

COMMANDER

Present arms. (The army present arms. The fanfare resumes the military music. The King moves away, theatrically with his staff)

CURTAIN

ACT II
SCENE 3

A square in Lisbon, which has just been ravaged by an earthquake. Many houses are destroyed or gravely damaged. In the back a church with some debris in front of the porch. The terrified inhabitants wander through rubble in despair. The troops of St. Hermandad are being used to reestablish order.

AT RISE, the inhabitants are wandering through the ruins. Religious songs and music can be heard nearing slowly.

1st INHABITANT

This is frightful! What a terrifying earthquake. My wife, where is my wife? Crushed under the rubble, alas!

2nd INHABITANT

My treasure!—Oh—where is my treasure? 900 douros that I had hidden in a wall. (To 1st Inhabitant) Imbecile! You'll find without difficulty another wife. Wives can easily be replaced, whereas treasures—

OFFICER OF ST. HERMANDAD

Silence!—And on your knees—Here is the Grand Inquisitor—(All kneel—the Grand Inquisitor enters followed by a cortege of worthy ecclesiastics. The Grand Inquisitor goes about the square blessing the victims)

GRAND INQUISITOR

(Contemplating the ruins) What a great and magnificent spectacle this earthquake is.

1st INHABITANT

My children perished, crushed.

2nd INHABITANT

My old mother was burned alive—

OFFICER OF ST. HERMANDAD

Silence!

GRAND INQUISITOR

Lucky day—for our eternal wellbeing—! Come, thank God! (Followed by worthy ecclesiastics—He gravely and slowly ascends the steps leading to the church.

Then resting upright as the others are kneeling—he turns toward the crowd and solemnly blesses them while the church is lit up) My brothers, let us rejoice and address to heaven gestures of grace! For the Lord has manifested himself to us today—his inexhaustible bounty. Be thankful to him sinners—for you have been turned away by a paternal warning from the way to damnation! The Eternal would have been able in his redoubtable right to reduce all Lisbon to dust, and if he chose not one of you would have survived. In short, God has destroyed on only three quarters of the city and a good portions of the sinners who inhabit it have been spared. Thank him for so much charity.

2nd INHABITANT

My treasure! My douros! Oh Lord return them to me, (He receives a blow from a pikeman)

GRAND INQUISITOR

My brothers, the city of Lisbon was another Sodom—another Gomorrah—it was the home of luxury, impurity, heresy and iniquity—Diabolic aberration! So as to lead the people to the right path, a war, an epidemic, an earthquake was necessary! God in His forbearance has chosen an earthquake, and what an earthquake. Truly he has spoiled us!

After this proof of Celestial Benevolence, we can't just content ourselves by addressing to our father prayers and canticles. We must do better to witness to him our gratitude and appease his just wrath. Burning candles won't suffice. Let's burn heretics, hardened sinners who by their crimes have very much justified the divine wrath. Let us organize a beautiful auto-da-fé.

ECCLESIASTIC

A noble and pious thought, Milord.

2nd ECCLESIASTIC

Fire purifies all—even souls. An auto-da-fé is evidently required.

INHABITANTS

Yes, yes, an auto-da-fé—a huge auto-da-fé. What joy, we are going to see burned people—a whole bunch of people. Long live the Inquisitor!

GRAND INQUISITOR

But above all, let's go on our knees before the altar of the one who is all goodness, all love! (The music resumes and the Grand Inquisitor followed by other worthy ecclesiastics enters the church whose doors close after them) (Candide and Pangloss enter from the rear, their clothes disordered and soiled)

CANDIDE

What a horrible catastrophe! Unfortunate city! Miserable inhabitants!

PANGLOSS

(Approaching from a house) How all things are linked together in an admirable bond! See, we were just shipwrecked, we are soaked and now, thanks to this providential earthquake, Lisbon has taken fire—which permits us to dry our clothes.

CANDIDE

Yes, but it was because of this earthquake that we shipwrecked in Lisbon harbor.

PANGLOSS

Evidently—all this is perfectly correct and admirably logical.

CANDIDE

You find this logical? You are easily satisfied. The train of events which brought us here seems to me, on the contrary, like a fantasy which borders on the incoherent! The glorious Monarch of Bulgaria had condemned me to be shot. I wasn't and it's the glorious Monarch, who vanquished by the Abares, was dethroned by his people.

PANGLOSS

A fair return of things down here.

CANDIDE

I never expected to see you again. Then escaping from the Bulgars I embarked for Lisbon—my boat was shipwrecked in the harbor, caused by the earthquake and who do I see, floating like me on a plank after having, like me, been shipwrecked in Lisbon harbor. My dear and venerable master of Philosophy, Doctor Pangloss—and in what condition, great God! That bandage on your eye! You were wounded in that terrible war that I, through God's grace, spent in prison?

PANGLOSS

Alas! Candide, I was the victim of a scourge worse than war: love!

CANDIDE

Can it be? Love, tender love, consoler of mankind? It's true it only got me several kicks in the ass.

PANGLOSS

Indeed it gives terrible kicks; but it must be so, since everything is ordered in nature for the greatest good of humanity.

CANDIDE

That's why I hope soon to see Miss Cunegonde again.

PANGLOSS

That my dear Candide—is impossible. Cunegonde has ceased to live.

CANDIDE

What are you saying?

PANGLOSS

I say that Westphalia having been invaded by the Bulgarian army, Cunegonde died, disemboweled, after having been violated by a Bulgarian soldier, as the Baroness also died, having been cut into small pieces, and the Baron who had his head split open by a blow from an ax.

CANDIDE

(Shivering) This is terrible—this is horrible—dead! Cunegonde, my darling Cunegonde, the most beautiful of women! Pangloss, my good Pangloss—support me—(He trembles and falls into Pangloss' arms)

SAILOR

(Who is picking through the ruins) Oh—what luck—a

treasure! (Discovering a box of coins) At a glance—It must be at least 600 douros. Long live the storm! Long live the earthquake! (Dancing with joy) Ah, we're going to be able to amuse ourselves. Women are mine! I'm thirsty—I want to drink! Let them pour me wine—I've got the money (Clicking his douros)

PANGLOSS

(While occupied with Candide who swoons) My friend, this is not good. You lack universal reason—you spend your time ill.

SAILOR

Head and blood! I am a sailor and born in Batavia, I trampled four times on the cross in our voyages to Japan—You've really found your man with your universal reason! Universal reason! Here—there it is (Pointing to his gold) Goodbye, I am going on a spree! (He throws the empty box on the ground after having put the gold in his pockets. He leaves)

1st INHABITANT

My treasure! Who will return my treasure to me? (He notices the box) Oh heavens, there it is! (Opening the box feverishly) Empty! (He utters a scream)

OFFICER OF ST. HERMANDAD

Silence! (He shuts him up with blows of the pike)

2ᴺᴰ INHABITANT

Here is a good place for us to see the cortege pass.

3ᴿᴰ INHABITANT

It will be the most beautiful auto-da-fé of the season.

4ᵀᴴ INHABITANT

Yes, but this won't change anything. Lisbon is in ruins and 30,000 people have perished!

PANGLOSS

(Having placed Candide on a bit of rubble where he silently weeps) And then? In what respect does this disturb the harmony of causes and effects? You are making a scandal with your earthquake! This phenomena is not a new thing. I imagine. The city of Lima received the same jolts in America, last year. Same cause, same effect! If there was a volcano in Lisbon it could not be otherwise. And you wouldn't want a volcano, all the same, that was unable to do its work as a volcano? Believe me my friends events are linked together with an irrefutable logic—and all is for the best in the best of worlds!

(While Pangloss orates in the midst of the inhabitants, the Grand Inquisitor mingles amongst the idlers and listens. Then, approaching the Philosopher—)

GRAND INQUISITOR

Pardon, sir—who are you?

PANGLOSS

(Proudly) Doctor Pangloss, Philosopher, professor of Metaphysical, Theological, Cosmological, Pedagogical Philosophy.

GRAND INQUISITOR

(Severely) You find everything is for the best?

PANGLOSS

Yes, everything is for the best, in the best of all possible worlds.

GRAND INQUISITOR

Apparently, sir, you don't believe in original sin—for if everything is for the best there would be neither fall nor punishment?

PANGLOSS

I ask your pardon very humbly sir, but the fall of man and the curse are not incompatible with my system.

GRAND INQUISITOR

That will suffice, sir! (To a staffer of Saint Hermandad) This Philosopher will do very well in our auto-da-fé. Go dress him for the ceremony. (Pangloss is led aside. As this happens the Grand Inquisitor addresses himself to Candide) And you, sir, who are you? It seems to me that you were listening to this Philosopher with an air of approval?

CANDIDE

He is my master and my friend—the only man with whom I can speak of Cunegonde. I wish to share his fate.

GRAND INQUISITOR

Ah, very well! (To a staff member) Lead this gentleman. And let them whip him in cadence during the auto-da-fé—In cadence, you hear—? Besides we will have a very lovely musical accompaniment. (The music can be heard. The procession comes forward, first the musicians—then the officers and soldiers of Saint Hermandad—Then the worthy Ecclesiastics. The "relapsed" march one by one with the Sanbenito and the paper mitre—each holds a candle in his hand—Then monks chanting—Then soldiers of Saint Hermandad—Pangloss is the last of the relapsed, Candide ends the march boxed in by two staffers armed with clubs.)

INHABITANT

This is superb! Without the earthquake we would never have seen such a beautiful auto-da-fé.

FEMALE INHABITANT

Oh—how amusing this is.

ANOTHER FEMALE INHABITANT

There's not a single pretty fellow in the whole lot!

FEMALE INHABITANT

Pardon—There's that one there—(Pointing to Candide) Are they going to burn him, too? (A female can be heard screaming off)

INHABITANT

What's happening?

FEMALE INHABITANT

Nothing—a lady just found herself unwell on her balcony.

ANOTHER FEMALE INHABITANT

Who is it?

FEMALE INHABITANT

A guest of the Grand Inquisitor it seems. She's wrong to be so upset these folks are going to be burned— As for me, I will go add my faggot to the fire. (The "relapsed" kneel—the Grand Inquisitor appears on the top of the church steps)

OFFICER OF ST. HERMANDAD

Come on, on your knees! The Grand Inquisitor is going to honor you with a sermon.

GRAND INQUISITOR

My brothers—you are going to be burned. It's for your benefit that the Holy Inquisition has so decided. But it's also for the benefit of everyone. When you are in the flames, remind yourself, that this beautiful auto-da-fé which you have the honor to take part in will possibly earn the pardon of the Very Highest—and we will be spared another earthquake! I have no need to remind the public of the sins you have committed (In a strident voice) To the pyre!

CROWD

To the pyre! To the pyre! (They lead the relapsed— Meanwhile Candide is being whipped in cadence. As he screams very loud he is taken off but his screams can still be heard)

GRAND INQUISITOR

Next! (It's the turn of Pangloss but for some time thunder has been heard and rain begins to fall) Ah— see our Philosopher. Well sir, what do you think of all this? Is it all for the best in the best of all possible worlds?—Think, that you are going to be burned.

PANGLOSS

Milord, you've just said yourself that we will be burned for our greatest personal benefit and at the same time for the greatest general benefit. What an admirable demonstration of my system! And how not to think that all is for the best in the best of all worlds where one sees that to prevent earthquake it suffices to burn a few people at a small fire—(The rain increases)

OFFICER

(To the Grand Inquisitor) Milord, the pyre just went out under the rain. Impossible to relight it.

GRAND INQUISITOR

Then instead of burning this Philosopher—hang him. (As he utters these words the ground begins to shake. Walls crumble. The inhabitants run away. Uproar. The Grand Inquisitor and his supporters flee. Before the curtain falls the inhabitants are running in every direction some carrying boxes, some leading children—The

Grand Inquisitor and his police flee like the others; some churchmen have removed their soutane the better to run unhampered—Then pass a surgeon and two porters bearing the lifeless body of Pangloss. He still has a rope around his neck. Then, a moment later Candide walking pitifully, bent double and supported by the old woman. His two hands grasp his back and he appears to be in great pain.)

OLD WOMAN

My son, take courage—And come with me.

CURTAIN

ACT II
SCENE 4

A magnificent room—all gilded—with furniture in brocade—vases, etc.

PANGLOSS

That old woman has taken care of us admirably, my dear Candide—Here I am revived and you are walking more easily—you can even sit down.

CANDIDE

Yes—taking precautions. (Sitting painfully on a sofa)

PANGLOSS

Ah, my poor friend, you really suffered.

CANDIDE

The fact is I have no luck. I've lost Cunegonde and I spend my youth being whipped.

PANGLOSS

The universal equilibrium restores all. You've been cured by the ointments of the old woman—and splendidly dressed through her care. Anyway, what are your misfortunes compared to mine? As for me, I was hanged.

CANDIDE

Yes, but you didn't lose Cunegonde.

PANGLOSS

I was hanged and that's really something. It's true I was capable of being burned. Still thanks to the executor of great works who had badly knotted the rope, thanks to a surgeon who wanted to dissect me—and who restored me to life by making a critical incision, and thanks to this old woman, and thanks to you my dear Candide, I was saved and here we are reunited in this magnificent place where we have every reason to thank the Metaphysical—Theological—Cosmological—Pedagogical system which gives proof that all is for the best in the best of all possible worlds.

CANDIDE

We are perhaps—not yet at the end of our troubles: think that we are still in Lisbon, that the Inquisitor could find us—All this makes me uneasy—Without a doubt that old woman is helpful but why doesn't she ever answer my questions—? Why don't we even know where we are—?

PANGLOSS

What's it matter since we are so well off—

CANDIDE

We would be better off if Cunegonde were with us (The old woman appears supporting a veiled, richly dressed woman)

OLD WOMAN

Raise this veil.

CANDIDE

(Obeying) Oh! Cunegonde! (He faints)

PANGLOSS

Ah—for goodness sakes—

OLD WOMAN

Quick—help these poor children—(to Pangloss) Do something, you old blockhead (They douse the two lovers with spirit waters)

PANGLOSS

Let's unhook her. I think that is what's best to do. (He unhooks her) What a throat! Miss Cunegonde has improved since we saw her last.

CANDIDE

(Coming to—in a weak voice) Cunegonde! You, here!

CUNEGONDE

(Coming to) Candide! At last, I see you again! (To Pangloss) Say there! Have you quite finished old fool! (She pushes him away then recognizes him) Pangloss!

PANGLOSS

Yes, indeed! The Doctor Pangloss—your professor. I am triumphing—my philosophy carries it off. These lovers that all things separated must find each other again. They've found each other—that's the proof.

CANDIDE

(To Cunegonde) What—is it you? You are living? They told me you were violated? They didn't disembowel you?

CUNEGONDE

Yes indeed, but one doesn't always die from these two

accidents.

CANDIDE

But why are you in Portugal? And how did you know that I was here? And by what strange adventure have we found each other again in this house?

CUNEGONDE

Here—but we'll talk better over dinner (To old woman) Serve us supper! (The old woman obeys) First of all, I was in my bed and sleeping deeply when heaven rained and sent Bulgarians in our beautiful castle. A huge Bulgarian, six feet tall, abused me—

CANDIDE

Skip that, my darling Cunegonde—That detail makes me ill.

CUNEGONDE

I screamed, I struggled, I scratched, I tried to tear out the eyes of that huge Bulgarian—

CANDIDE

Ah, that makes me feel better.

CUNEGONDE

Yes, but that brute gave me a blow with the knife in my left flank whose scar I still bear.

CANDIDE

Indeed, I hope to see it.

CUNEGONDE

You shall see it. A Bulgarian Captain entered. He saw me all bloody and avenged me by killing the soldier on my body. Then he dressed me and led me as a prisoner of war to his quarters. I washed the few clothes that he had. I cooked for him, he found me very pretty and I won't deny that he had white—soft skin. Yet little wit and philosophy—You could see plainly he hadn't been raised by Doctor Pangloss.

PANGLOSS

(Bowing) Thanks—

CUNEGONDE

At the end of three months the Captain sold me to a Jew, Don Issachar who traded in Portugal and who passionately loved the ladies. I resisted him better than the Bulgarian soldier. A person of honor can be violated once but her virtue increases. This Jew to tame me brought me to this country house.

CANDIDE

We are in the house of this man.

CUNEGONDE

You are in it.

CANDIDE

(Anxiously) You are still resisting him right?

CUNEGONDE

Hold on—The Grand Inquisitor noticed me one day at Mass—He observed me a lot—

CANDIDE

You make me tremble—

CUNEGONDE

Ah, it's hard being a woman—and wrong to judge them severely, inconsiderately. I've had to accommodate myself to an agreement reached between the Jew and the Inquisitor. The Jew disposes of the house and my person Monday, Tuesday, and on the Sabbath; the Inquisitor is at home here on the other days of the week. It hasn't been without quarrels, for often it was undecided whether the night of Saturday to Sunday belonged to the old law or the new—that is to say, the

Jew or the Inquisitor.

CANDIDE

These details break my heart.

CUNEGONDE

Then they had an auto-da-fé. The Inquisitor did me the honor of inviting me to it. I was very well placed. But what was my surprise, my terror, my trouble, when I recognized Pangloss among the relapsed, when I saw you, o my friend—stripped, totally naked—being whipped. That was the completion of horror, of consternation, of sorrow, of despair—I uttered a scream—and I fainted.

CANDIDE

Unlucky Cunegonde!

CUNEGONDE

I tell you truthfully, that your skin is still whiter and of a brightness more perfect than that of my Bulgarian Captain.

CANDIDE

Darling Cunegonde.

CUNEGONDE

At last, when you were indeed whipped, I came to. The old woman that I charged to bring you here and care for you faithfully executed that commission. But how many trials! Ah, I no longer think of the philosophy of Doctor Pangloss.

PANGLOSS

(Glass in hand) What your beautiful castle has been completely destroyed, your family was massacred, you were raped and disemboweled, you were shared by a Jew and the Grand Inquisitor, Candide was whipped in cadence, I was hung—and when we find each other together again in this beautiful room, in the act of supping with the best music in the world, you say that optimism is a philosophic error—Ah, indeed—for goodness sake—I don't understand you.

OLD WOMAN

(To Pangloss aside)

I think that these young people don't want to discuss Philosophy—especially at this moment! Let's leave them! All will be for the best, believe me, when we no longer get in their way (They leave)

CANDIDE

Alone at last!

CUNEGONDE

Here's a happy moment—

CANDIDE

You recall our kiss in the little woods?

CUNEGONDE

It still burns on my lips. But it must boil in you, too, my dear Candide, since that kiss cost you, alas, many kicks in the ass on the part of my poor father.

CANDIDE

It is worth it to me, moreover, because a single cause can have several effects: to be with the Bulgars, to be with the Portuguese—But it's not too much to pay for a joy like this!

CUNEGONDE

(Sitting on the sofa) Come, hold me again—Let's exchange a second kiss—This time we can do it—with impunity—

CANDIDE

Yes, no one can bother us and I no longer risk anything—(They sit on the sofa and embrace)

DON ISSACHAR

(Noticing the couple with fury) By the God of Israel!

CUNEGONDE

Heavens! The Jew!

DON ISSACHAR

What Galilean bitch—isn't the Inquisitor enough? Must this rascal share you with me, too. (Drawing a long dagger from his belt and rushing towards Candide. Candide draws his sword and without speaking runs the Jew through—who falls dead)

CUNEGONDE

Holy Virgin! A man slain in my home. If the police come we are lost. It's my fault—Today is Saturday—and it was the Jew's day—What shall we do?

CANDIDE

Let's consult Pangloss! (Opening the door and calling the Philosopher) Pangloss enters.

CUNEGONDE

Candide has just killed Don Issachar who pretended to prevent him from embracing me. This is horrible! What is going to become of us?

PANGLOSS

It's a thrilling drama! (To Candide) Not important. You will be acquitted—

CANDIDE

You think so?

PANGLOSS

I am sure of it. Find a lawyer and he won't have any trouble demonstrating that this murder was willed by universal reason—husbands, lovers, spouses and masters have the right to kill—and, besides that the Holy Inquisitor must be grateful to you for having simplified his work in suppressing this Hebrew promised to a future auto-da-fé. You will see the judge will congratulate you.

CUNEGONDE

Oh—thanks my dear Pangloss—you reassure me.

PANGLOSS

(Withdrawing) At your disposal.

CANDIDE

Let's forget this incident and make up for last time. (They sit back down on the sofa and hold each other again. Midnight strikes)

GRAND INQUISITOR

(Entering) Midnight is striking—It is now Sunday and the beautiful Cunegonde is mine (Noticing the couple entwined) Hell and Damnation! (Noticing the stretched out cadaver) What's going on?

CANDIDE

(To Cunegonde) If this Holy man calls for help he will infallibly have me burned. He will do the same to you my dear Cunegonde.

CUNEGONDE

Then—?

CANDIDE

Then there's nothing to consider. I'm busy with killing—let's kill this one, too—(With a blow of his sword he runs the Grand Inquisitor through)

CUNEGONDE

Here's another one indeed—There's no relief. We are excommunicated—our last hour has come—What have you done, you who were born so sweet—to kill in two minutes a Jew and the Grand Inquisitor—

CANDIDE

My pretty miss—when one is amorous, jealous and whipped by the Inquisitor one no longer knows oneself any more.

PANGLOSS

(Entering) Another thrilling crime? That makes two of them—that's too many.

The OLD WOMAN

Jesus! Mary!

CANDIDE

(To Cunegonde) Decidedly, my darling—I don't have luck each time I embrace you.

PANGLOSS

What's done is done—and there's no going over it. Something tells me anyway that this is just a wrong for a benefit—The Metaphysical—Theological—

OLD WOMAN

I don't know about that but I have some advice to give you—and this is it. Let's get out of here—and as rapidly as possible.

CANDIDE

I don't cling to remaining here—

OLD WOMAN

There are three Andalousian horses in the stable. Give orders for them to be prepared by our valet, the half breed Cacambo, a man of wit, subtle and resourceful. He will know all the ways, all the tricks. He also knows the fences and can sell the diamonds and the trinkets that Madame obtained from the generosity of the Jew and the Inquisitor. He will lead us to Cadiz from where we will leave for Buenos Aires.

PANGLOSS

Excellent idea! America is a very fine country—and all is for the best in the best of all possible worlds.

OLD WOMAN

Let's leave quickly—There is just time—and let's leave by the back door—I hear the patrol of the Holy Hermandad passing in the street—(She drags them off and they leave by the left—striding over the bodies. As soon as they are gone. There's rapping on the door at the right)

VOICE

Open to Saint Hermandad! Open—! Break down the

door! (The door falls—staffers enter preceded by a Jesuit)

JESUIT

That honorable stool pigeon who warned us spoke truly. Here are two men murdered. (Going to Don Issachar) A Jew—no importance—to the sewers—(Two staffers take the body of the Jew and toss it out the window)

JESUIT

(Considering the other body) Oh heaven! Milord the Grand Inquisitor—Quickly—search the house—arrest everybody—run to the nearest church ring the bell and announce in the streets a new auto-da-fé to pay for the murder of Milord the Grand Inquisitor (The staffers rush out. The Jesuit remains alone near the body of the Inquisitor—Kneeling—joining his hands he mutters a prayer. Then having removed the Episcopal ring from the dead man's finger he places it on his own hand, rises and says) Now I am the Grand Inquisitor!

(While the curtain falls one hears the bell ring and voices shouting in the street)

VOICES

Auto-da-fé! Auto-da-fé!

CURTAIN

ACT III
SCENE 5

Buenos Aires: the Hall of Honor in Palace of the Governor Don Fernando d'Ibarra y Figueroa y Mascarenes y Lampourdes y Souza—The Hall is vast, hung with magnificent draperies—of gold, red, blue and green.

In the doorway some alguazils appear dressed in purple and gold and hold pikestaffs in hand. In the milieu, a crowd of petitioners, male and female, standing in modest poses.

ALGUAZIL

(Announcing after having rapped the floor with his halberd) His Excellency, the Governor of Buenos Aires Don Fernando d'Ibarra y Figueroa y Mascarenes y Lampourdes y Souza (The Governor makes his entry. He's in the same colors as the Alguazils but more magnificent—more golden. He holds his head high, nose in the air—a black, ebony mustache—His manner is exalted, he affects an air of extreme impertinence. He leans on a tall cane in the manner of the mignons of Henry III. A martial music from brass horns accompanies his entry. He slowly tours the room without looking at anyone—head pointed toward heaven, followed by a secretary in black and by alguazils who rap the floor with their halberds at every step—he sits on an armchair that much resembles a throne on a platform reached by three steps)

SECRETARY

The Audience of His Excellency the Governor—is opened.

GOVERNOR

Read the petitions—in résumé, of course—

SECRETARY

(Reading) Elizondo Fernández, old man of sixty-eight and faithful servant of Your High Excellence complains of having been molested by the alguazils who drank his wine, emptied his cash box and tousled his daughter.

GOVERNOR

Bad wit! A 1,000-douros fine to teach him to accuse without proof the supporters of the State. Next—!

SECRETARY

The two wretches who didn't bow to Your Excellency's carriage yesterday ask for mercy.

GOVERNOR

To the gallows!

SECRETARY

Morales, Concepción, mother of eleven children, hasn't paid the tax. She invokes the provisions of the law for large families.

GOVERNOR

Let her furniture be seized and sold. And then?

SECRETARY

The inhabitants of villages devastated by the enemy ask for lodging and complain of the lack of concern on the part of public authorities in their regard.

GOVERNOR

Ah! They complain and they ask for lodging—Well—They shall have it—in prison!

SECRETARY

Bustros, Domenico.

MAN'S VOICE IN CROWD

Here!

SECRETARY

Silence—versus Apeztequi, Conchita

WOMAN'S VOICE

I am here.

SECRETARY

Silence! (The Governor at first frowns. Then he looks at the young woman who appears very pretty. She smiles coquettishly at the Governor who curls his mustache)

GOVERNOR

Come forward! (The man and the woman approach the Governor; she more and more coquettish and provoking. The Governor very friendly) Of whom do you complain, my child?

YOUNG WOMAN

Of no one, Excellency, I am perfectly happy under the

beneficent administration of Your Excellency.

MAN

It's I who complain. I found my wife in a gallant conversation with an officer. (The Governor raises his cane with an air of impatience)

SECRETARY

Silence!

MAN

I demand justice, Excellency, against this adulterous woman. (Another gesture by the Governor)

SECRETARY

Silence!

GOVERNOR

Take this man away. He will receive fifty blows with the baton for having raised his voice in my presence without being questioned (They lead the husband away. The Governor rises, goes to the young woman who speaks very close to him, smiling)

GOVERNOR

The audience is closed! Make everyone leave. You will

bring me those people who arrived from Spain this morning; I will question them soon! (The alguazils hustle the crowd out. The Governor takes the hand of the young woman and leads her out to the left. A door opens—enter Candide, Cunegonde and Pangloss)

ALGUAZIL

Wait here. His Excellency the Governor will receive you soon after his Council of Ministers leaves (Goes out)

CANDIDE

I persist in thinking, beautiful Cunegonde that we would have acted more wisely by not presenting ourselves here. It's really putting ourselves into the wolf's throat.

CUNEGONDE

Why's that? I am baroness with seventy-two quarters. Don Fernando d' Ibarra y Figueroa y Mascarenes y Lampourdes y Souza is a noble hidalgo, he will grant me the protection that he owes to a woman of his caste.

CANDIDE

These hidalgos are highly inflammable. When they protect a woman as beautiful as you it's always with an ulterior motive of extracting a guilty recompense.

CUNEGONDE

Dear Candide, I've been violated by two Bulgarians, by a Jew and by an Inquisitor; I know men and I march through peril like a grenadier under fire—without trembling—Life has its necessities.

OLD WOMAN

Now there's a sensible thing said, my beautiful miss. As the Moors say, what is written is written and we must accept our destiny.

PANGLOSS

Moreover everything being well and arranged by the universal harmony, it can result only in the best of events under the most calamitous appearances.

CUNEGONDE

After all, I've been so horribly treated in the old world that whatever may happen to me in the new cannot be any worse!

OLD WOMAN

You complain! Alas, you've never endured misfortunes such as mine.

CUNEGONDE

I find you very funny, my dear, to pretend to be more unfortunate than I. Unless you were violated by three Bulgarians, and you get two knife slashes in your bowels, had two of your castles demolished, had two mothers and two fathers butchered before your eyes, had two of your lovers whipped in an auto-da-fé—I don't see that you could beat me.

OLD WOMAN

Miss, if I were to show you the part of my body on which I sit, you wouldn't speak as you do and you would suspend your judgment.

CUNEGONDE

Really? Show me then; I've seen plenty of others.

OLD WOMAN

Because you contemplate my bloodshot eyes, bordered with scarlet, my nose which touches my chin and my dishpan hands you imagine I have always been ugly and that I've always been a servant—Undeceive yourself! Such as you see me, I am the daughter of Pope Urban X and the Princess Palestrini—Palestrina—

PANGLOSS

(Displaying skepticism in bad taste) Funicula—

Funicula.

OLD WOMAN

They brought me up until I was 14 in a palace compared to which all your German castles would only have served as a stable. I grew in grace, beauty, talent—My throat formed—what a throat!—My eyes got larger—what eyes—My eyebrows grew arched—what eyebrows! My bearing became majestic.

CANDIDE

What bearing!

OLD WOMAN

The Prince of Massa Carrara, handsome like the day, sharp as a needle, rich like Croesus, demanded my hand—What a Prince!

PANGLOSS

And what a hand!

OLD WOMAN

I experienced joy—when an old Marquise, who had been the Mistress of my Prince invited him to take chocolate with her—he died in two hours in the midst of terrible convulsions.

PANGLOSS

The Turks have the worst coffee. The Italians prefer the worst chocolate. Each people has its traditions—all equally respectable.

OLD WOMAN

That chocolate was the sign of my misfortunes. To pull me out of despair my mother wanted to take me by boat to Greta where she owned some very beautiful property. Hardly at sea, a Moroccan corsair from Sale pounced on our galley. We were captured and made to submit to outrages that they call The Last! Alas, they weren't the last, for they renewed them frequently in the course of a captivity led that to Azov during the siege of that city by the Russians. The Turks defending the place reduced to famine decided to cut from each of the women—a slice of flesh from the lower back—to assure the survival of the army.

CUNEGONDE

O heaven!

OLD WOMAN

Exactly! Since that time I've only had one cheek to sit on—Doesn't it seem to you that for the daughter of the Pope, that was a misfortune sufficiently dramatic and that I have some rights to support my candidacy to the title of the most unhappy creature of human kind?

PANGLOSS

Observe, nevertheless, that half your ass remains to you and you could no longer have it all. You must thank Providence and render homage to the benevolence of nature which allowed you to preserve half of that which you might have lost in its entirety.

ALGUAZIL

(Opening both doors) His Excellency the Governor Don Fernando d'Ibarra y Figueroa y Mascarenes y Lampourdes y Souza. Rise and assume a respectful attitude! (The Governor goes to sit on his throne and immediately his attention is attracted to the person of Miss Cunegonde whom he examines with great sympathy and interest)

GOVERNOR

Come closer and be so kind as to expose to me— the object of your—request. (Cunegonde, Candide, Pangloss and the old Woman approach)

PANGLOSS

Excellency, these honorable persons and myself—(The Governor raises his cane in sign of impatience)

SECRETARY

Silence!

GOVERNOR

(To Cunegonde) Please to sit down, beautiful lady—and tell me in what way it will be possible for to be of use to you.

CUNEGONDE

Excellency, I am the baroness of Thunder-ten-Tronchk—and I have seventy-two quarters of nobility. (The Governor bows) Constrained by the misfortune of the times and a string of adventures that would take too long to tell you here, I've been exiled from the land of my birth; I settled first at Lisbon for a while—then the desire took me to visit the beautiful countries whose government and happiness your Excellency presides over with so much majesty and genius. (The Governor bows again)

GOVERNOR

(Twirling his mustache furiously and casting burning glances at Cunegonde) A person of quality and made like you doesn't address in vain a noble hidalgo. From this moment you are under my protection—But would you present to me these persons who accompany you.

CUNEGONDE

I excuse myself, Excellency for not having as yet fulfilled this duty. Here's Captain Candide, Baron of Thunder-ten-Tronchk who served with valor in the Bulgarian army. (Candide bows to the Governor who makes him a little protective sign with his hand) Doctor Pangloss the great Philosopher—master of the Metaphysical—Theological—Cosmological Pedagogy—(Pangloss leans like an arc of a circle)

GOVERNOR

I don't like Philosophers.

PANGLOSS

Allow me, Excellency (Sign of the cane by Governor)

SECRETARY

Silence.

CUNEGONDE

And here's The Princess Palestrini—Palestrina—daughter of Pope Urban X and a servant of no importance (Old Woman prostrates herself)

GOVERNOR

Get up, daughter of no importance to Pope Urban

X, and turn towards the wall. Your mustached face offends my sight. (The old Woman obeys. Then the Governor turns with a threatening air toward Candide) Captain Candide would you be the husband of the noble Baroness?

CANDIDE

Excellency—

CUNEGONDE

(Cutting him off) Excellency, my cousin Candide having been able to prove only seventy-one quarters of nobility and the rest of his family tree having been ruined through the troubled times, it was impossible for me to marry him—despite a tender inclination that draws us toward each other.

CANDIDE

But in this new world where differences in nobility are envisaged by a larger spirit—Miss Cunegonde ought to do me the honor of marrying me and I entreat Your Excellency to deign to marry us.

GOVERNOR

Captain Candide your particular interests must be forced to give way to those of the country. I incorporate you into my army with your grade and I order you to go inspect your company—which my secretary will commission you in. You will leave tomorrow for Paraguay where I am at war with the Jesuit fathers.

CANDIDE

Excellency couldn't I just marry Miss Cunegonde?

GOVERNOR

Not a word! You can go get prepared. Also the Philosopher and the Pope's daughter—(The Alguazils make Candide, Pangloss and the old Woman leave) Beautiful lady—noble Spaniards—and even men who are neither noble, nor Spanish but who exercise authority are not accustomed to beat around the bush in matters of love. I love you, I want you and you will be my wife.

CUNEGONDE

Your wife, Excellency.

GOVERNOR

If you are fussy, that detail is entirely indifferent to me so long as you give yourself to me. I will marry you tonight in the face of the church—or otherwise, whatever is pleasing to your charms.

CUNEGONDE

Excellency, your demand flatters me infinitely and the

delicacy with which it is expressed touches me more than I know how to say—Nevertheless, in a circumstance so important to me, I feel the need to think it over, to meditate, and to ask the advice of my Patron Saints—as well as that venerable woman who accompanies me.

GOVERNOR

I give you a quarter of an hour—(To Alguazil) Make the daughter of the Pope come. (To Cunegonde) In a quarter of an hour I will return to find you. (Kissing her hand) Beautiful lady—take me as the most humble, the most submissive, and the most respectful of your servants. (Cunegonde curtsies—The Governor leaves majestically. The Alguazil brings in the old Woman)

CUNEGONDE

Good old Woman—here I am engaged in a new adventure, and one more time it will probably be necessary to be the plaything of masculine lust.

OLD WOMAN

I understood. I observed the Governor was making eyes.

CUNEGONDE

Eyes! He intends to marry me this evening, legitimately or not.

OLD WOMAN

I am ravished to learn this good news.

CUNEGONDE

Why it's a terrifying calamity! Candide, my darling Candide—Am I going to be forced to be unfaithful to him one more time?

OLD WOMAN

Miss, you have seventy-two quarters of nobility and not one Spanish copper. It's necessary for you to be the wife of the greatest lord in America who has a very beautiful mustache. Are you priding yourself on an unflinching fidelity? You were violated by the Bulgarians, a Jew, an Inquisitor have seen your beauties. Wrongs give rights. Marry the Governor—you will make your fortune and what's more that of Captain Candide who won't fail to rapidly become Colonel—then General, and better still perhaps.

CUNEGONDE

Is that your advice?

OLD WOMAN

By Saint Jacques of Compostola, our lady of Atocha, and good Saint Anthony that decision seems to me the only one that conforms to reason—and morality—

properly—understood—(At this moment Candide and Cacambo enter, very agitated—followed by Doctor Pangloss who has lost most of his calm)

CANDIDE

Alas, beautiful Cunegonde—here's yet another catastrophe ready to break upon us.

CACAMBO

And how! It's prison and worse—if one doesn't act quickly.

CUNEGONDE

(To Cacambo) Speak, Cacambo.

CACAMBO

A ship has just arrived in port bearing an Alcade in pursuit of the murderers of Milord the Grand Inquisitor.

CUNEGONDE

Oh heaven!

CACAMBO

Our description has been given—We will be arrested in a quarter of an hour.

OLD WOMAN

(To Cunegonde) God be praised! We have a quarter of an hour. In a quarter of an hour you will be saved since you have only to seek refuge in the arms of the Governor—

CUNEGONDE

(Docile) Candide, my dear Candide.

OLD WOMAN

He must take flight without losing an instant (To Candide) Flee then or in an hour you are going to be burned.

CANDIDE

Never without Cunegonde.

OLD WOMAN

He must. Miss Cunegonde, thanks to her seventy-two quarters of nobility is protected by the Governor—who witnesses great consideration for her.

CANDIDE

Indeed I've seen how he considers her. He considers her as his property.

CUNEGONDE

My dear Candide, I permit you to resist until the last extremity.

CANDIDE

Yes—but after the last extremity? (Cunegonde makes a gesture expressing fatality)

PANGLOSS

Nothing can happen which is not conceived and willed by universal wisdom. Instead of being alarmed, for there are no effects without causes, and causes emanate from the natural order, which, as you will know, realize, and achieve the same perfection.

CANDIDE

Oh my darling Cunegonde, must I again abandon you—? What will become of you?

CACAMBO

Miss will become what she can—women are never embarrassed by themselves—God will provide. Let's run for it.

PANGLOSS

Eh, yes! Let's run for it!

OLD WOMAN

Run for it!

CUNEGONDE

Run, my friend!

CANDIDE

Where will I go without you? (To Cacambo) Where do you pretend to take me?

CACAMBO

By Saint Jacques of Compostola you were going to go make war on the Jesuits—Come do it for them. They will be charmed to have a Captain from the Bulgarian Army. You will make a prodigious fortune.

PANGLOSS

Let's run for it!

OLD WOMAN

Run!

CUNEGONDE

Run, dear Candide.

CANDIDE

I'm off!—Goodbye, then, darling Cunegonde—!

CUNEGONDE

Goodbye, goodbye, my good Candide. (He kisses her hand passionately and leaves dragged by Pangloss and Cacambo and pushed by the old Woman)

OLD WOMAN

Ouf! Now we are rid of them! Now be everything to the Governor.

ALGUAZIL

(Announcing) His Excellency—The Governor (Enter the Governor still as majestic and Imposing)

GOVERNOR

(To Cunegonde) Well—

CUNEGONDE

Let it be according to your will!

GOVERNOR

I was sure of it (He makes a sign with his cane—The Alguazils open a door and The Chaplain enters followed by servants—The Governor escorts Cunegonde out in a grand procession.)

OLD WOMAN

At last—here we are in a stable situation.

CURTAIN

ACT IV
SCENE 6

Eldorado—A magnificent tropical sun. Gigantic trees. Marvelous flowers—In the middle a vast clearing with golden soil. In the back two handsome buildings.

CANDIDE

Where are we? And what strange company did the storm throw us in?

PANGLOSS

In any case, we are much better here than in Buenos Aires.

CANDIDE

Yes, but I've again lost Miss Cunegonde!

PANGLOSS

Bah! We'll find her again. All our past adventures proceeded from the universal logic, like those which are reserved for us in this unknown country. Isn't that your opinion, subtle Cacambo?

CACAMBO

My opinion is that the universal logic would do well to guide us to a well provisioned inn.

CANDIDE

(Bitterly) The universal logic has doubtless too much to do to concern itself about our modest selves. It is occupied with unleashing wars, massacres, earthquakes, fires, shipwrecks and cataclysms of all sorts which are part of the plan conceived by it with the end of insuring the happiness of humanity.

PANGLOSS

Its designs are impenetrable to common intelligences—Only philosophers—

CANDIDE

(Completely losing the notion of respect and shrugging his shoulders) Philosophers!—Here! This is what philosophers make me do! Philosophers!

CACAMBO

(To Candide) You are right. Here we are once again in a country of savages—and (looking around him) But say—not all that savage—Beautiful trees, magnificent flowers—buildings—all this has a very comfortable appearance—This is rich—Perhaps there'll be a way to get out of this here—And if we can only find someone to show us—Heavens—there's just what we need—These children playing—(Two children have entered magnificently dressed in gold brocade. They play with gold quoits)

PANGLOSS

These children seem to me to belong to a well off class of society. See how magnificent their clothes are.

CACAMBO

One would say they are dressed in real gold.

CANDIDE

Perhaps without knowing it we've entered the palace of the King of the country.

CACAMBO

For sure—This park—These children in gold—(The children go off playing—they've left several quoits on the ground) And this! (Picks up a quoit) Have a look at this—This shines like a 25,000-real coin—It's made of gold!

PANGLOSS

(Marveling) It's made of gold!

CANDIDE

(Also marveling) It's made of gold!

PANGLOSS

(Coldly pocketing the quoit) Gold is a chimera.

CACAMBO

(Protesting) Excuse me, my master!

PANGLOSS

(Pointing to quoits remaining on the ground) There are some others. (Pangloss and Candide fill their pockets with quoits)

CACAMBO

(Picking up a pebble) The pebbles also are of gold.

CANDIDE

And the soil itself!

CACAMBO

God be praised!—We are in the land of gold—

Eldorado—The famous Eldorado of which I've heard speak. My friends, our fortune is made. (They all fill their pockets with stones)

PANGLOSS

(To Candide, all the while gathering stones) Do you deny now the wisdom of the plans conceived by universal logic? There exists a country where you have only to bend down to pick up gold—and we are in that land—

CACAMBO

May that last! (The children return with other children and a bearded man smoking gold pipe. His clothes are of gold decorated with diamonds and precious stones. Other natives, similarly dressed follow at a distance.)

BEARDED MAN

What are you doing there, good folk squatting on the ground and jumping around like frogs? (Candide and the others turn around surprised and stand up)

CANDIDE

(To his companions) It's the King!

PANGLOSS

It's the King!

CACAMBO

It's the King!

CANDIDE

(Respectfully) Sire, I have the honor to return to Your Majesty these jewels their Royal Highnesses left on the way.

PANGLOSS

(To Cacambo)

This young Candide decidedly has no common sense.

CACAMBO

(Simply) Booby! (The Bearded Man considers Candide with astonishment mixed with pity. Then he looks at the others present and all break out in laughter)

MAN

They are mad men!

WOMAN

Or foreigners.

BEARDED MAN

Which is exactly the same thing. Rise, young man, you are in a free country where genuflections don't go. Young man there's a mistake. I am not the sovereign of this country which anyway does not possess a sovereign. I am a school master in the village and I am taking these little scamps who are the sons of brave citizens of no consequence—home to their parents. As for the stones on the road that you are presenting to me, you can keep them—They are of no value—

CANDIDE

Why it's gold.

CACAMBO

Here are emeralds.

PANGLOSS

These rubies—are they imitations?

BEARDED MAN

Indeed—here's gold—rubies and emeralds—At least that's how they are denominated in the jargon of the old world where you probably come from—I don't know by what miracle. Cast your eyes about you, you will see the soil of this country is entirely of the same substance.

CACAMBO

The country of gold—Indeed I said so!

BEARDED MAN

The country of gold and precious stones—You have only to lean down to take them—

CANDIDE

But no one leans down—?

BEARDED MAN

By Jove. It's much too easy. What gave value to these stones in your backward nations is their rarity. Here one doesn't know what to do with them. Look at these diamonds which shine on the ears of this pretty girl? The rings which hide the fingers of this opulent matron.

CACAMBO

They're here by millions, it's true.

BEARDED MAN

It's true and they're not worth a goat shit. Take them for a song and if you sing again take the opulent matron and her daughter. These ladies will make you a gift of their jewels and their persons.

CANDIDE

Can it be?

CACAMBO

Indeed, that's interesting!

PANGLOSS

Wasn't I telling you that all is for the best in the best of worlds? (The beautiful girl advances on Candide with an alluring air offering him a collar of pearls and a pair of earrings—Candide recoils)

CANDIDE

Oh! Cunegonde! Protect me! (The opulent matron empties all her rings into the extended hands of Cacambo)

CACAMBO

(Taking her by the waist) There's nothing to say it's a street in Cockagne. (Pangloss advances smiling toward the pretty girl rejected by Candide)

PRETTY GIRL

(Looking him over) Oh, no—not that one. (She moves off—The opulent matron advances toward Pangloss with an engaging air)

PANGLOSS

Oh no—not that one (He moves away)

CANDIDE

Oh Heaven! Where am I?

BEARDED MAN

You are in the territory of Eldorado—

CANDIDE

The land of riches.

BEARDED MAN

No—the land of poverty.

CANDIDE

Of poverty—in the midst of all this gold, of these precious stones?

BEARDED MAN

Neither gold nor precious stones make riches. With all this gold, with all these precious stones we are poor folks in comparison to the nations of the old continents who only have paper—(Lyrically) Ah, paper, precious paper, inestimable paper—paper on which one prints a simple number followed by a considerable number of zeroes—that's true riches—modern riches.

PANGLOSS

Why it seems to me that paper still has only value to the extent it represents gold.

BEARDED MAN

Error my, dear fellow! It was good before. Paper today has an intrinsic value—It is King, it is God—The Golden Calf had his time Long Live the Paper Calf. And if you had on you one of those slips of filthy paper which serve as exchange between civilized people you would be master of the land.

PANGLOSS

A scrap of paper—Why I have one of them—(Pulling a filthy paper from his pocket) Here's a note for a pound. (Sensation amidst the natives who push and shove to get a look at its exclamations) "A bank note"—"Paper money!"

BEARDED MAN

How filthy it is—how beautiful!

PRETTY GIRL

How filthy it is—how beautiful!

OPULENT MATRON

How filthy it is—how beautiful!

ALL THREE TOGETHER

How filthy it is—how beautiful!

BEARDED MAN

My dear fellow I can no longer leave you. We are going to do some business! And to begin with, we are going to make a party—Are you hungry?

PANGLOSS

Falling down hungry.

BEARDED MAN

Thirsty?

CACAMBO

Dying of thirst.

BEARDED MAN

Then to dinner! (To people) And the rest of you—let them hurry to serve a rich feast to these opulent strangers—possessors of a bank note. (The natives rush about at the Bearded Man's orders. One brings a table richly furnished with crystal plates—wines and liquors—in finely chiseled bottles) Milords, deign to take seats on these sofas cushioned with humming bird feathers, and deign to do us the honor of taking part in this modest repast. You are here in a poor town and the most expensive thing is mediocre. Excuse us—these brave folk offer you the best of what they have. (Designating the items as they are brought) You will have only four soups each garnished with two parrots a little twist of boiled beef weighing two hundred pounds, two roasted monkeys, here in this plate 300 humming birds and in this one 600 humming birds; here are ragouts perfumed with aromatic herbs and country pastries quite delicate.—I particularly recommend to you the liquors that the servants are busy pouring. It's alcohol from sugar cane—Nothing in common with your rot gut brandy from Europe which they extract from wood, paper, rags.

CACAMBO

(Marveling) All this for a pound and a half!—And they pretend life is expensive!

BEARDED MAN

Sit down, gentlemen (They all sit down with the bearded Man) Eat and drink to your fantasy. And while you eat and drink these brave folks are going to play you a little music and show you some country dances. (The musicians play as Candide and his companions stuff themselves. The dancers are very pretty and bustle about very agreeably. Then there's a ballet. After the ballet the dancers and musicians leave—and leave the diners alone)

CANDIDE

Truthfully, sir I don't know how to thank you for this magnificent hospitality and fairy-like feast that you've offered us.

BEARDED MAN

Don't thank me. We are too much honored to treat persons of your importance—who possess bank notes—as they deserve. Besides we have no merit. The dishes and liquors that we offered you here are in such abundance that we attach no importance to them.

CANDIDE

But what is this country blessed by heavens where everything is just the opposite of what happens elsewhere?

BEARDED MAN

This country, ancient homeland of the Incas has become a republic of a new type—a republic without laws.

PANGLOSS

(Indignant) Without laws! Is it possible that human beings can push perversity to the point that they deprive themselves of the salutary tutelage of laws to live in liberty at their fancy without constraint? Now there's a heresy that universal reason, admonishes—a conception absolutory prejudicial to human dignity.

BEARDED MAN

When I say "Without laws," I am exaggerating. We respect one law. It is forbidden for any inhabitant of the republic to ever leave its territory. As we are surrounded inaccessible rocks and precipices, we have always been sheltered from the rapacity of European nations who have an inconceivable madness for the stones and dirt of our land and who—to have it, would kill us to the last man. That's what has protected our innocence and our happiness. Here, citizens—everything belongs to all—the treasures, the fields, the houses—the food, the beverages and the women. Take, eat, drink, love—At the disposition of "usted."

PANGLOSS

But property?

BEARDED MAN

There is no property.

CANDIDE

Morality?

BEARDED MAN

There is no morality.

CACAMBO

Police?

BEARDED MAN

There are no police.

CANDIDE

Religion?

BEARDED MAN

There is no religion.

PANGLOSS

Government?

BEARDED MAN

There is no government.

CACAMBO

Administration?

BEARDED MAN

There is no administration.

PANGLOSS

So then—it's anarchy?

BEARDED MAN

Not at all—It's nothing.

PANGLOSS

This country is bizarre. It turns my ideas upside down and makes me think for the first time that all is not for the best.—And it works?

BEARDED MAN

No worse than elsewhere.

PANGLOSS

Why it's barbarism—a savage condition.

CACAMBO

If it's a savage condition, it's good.

CANDIDE

If Miss Cunegonde were near me, I would believe myself to be in an earthly paradise.

CACAMBO

In any case, it's a country where one isn't worried.

BEARDED MAN

One isn't worried—it's much worse—one's bored.

CANDIDE

What are you telling me? In this superb nature!

CACAMBO

Where you eat so well?

CANDIDE

Where the soil is gold, and the houses made of precious stone?

CACAMBO

Where there are so many beautiful girls?

BEARDED MAN

Well, yes—my friends—I am going to open my heart

to you. You are civilized, you come from outside, you have a Bank note—with you one can talk. Ah, you don't know what it is to live in eternal beatitude in an earthly paradise. Where you are allowed to eat, to drink, to make love and roll in gold. No more desires, no more struggles, no more emotions! The dull calm, the eternal blue imitating the perpetual happiness of a heaven without clouds—As for me I am an old revolutionary. My name is Martin. I am a Manichean philosopher. Since I've known the ropes, I spend my time proving everything is evil. I am the eternal antagonist, the eternal destroyer. And it happens that here I have nothing to destroy, everything works like clockwork, no one says a word, and everybody is of the same opinion—And as for me, I am becoming sentimental, merciful, idiotic—I disgust myself—Ah, how did I come to be in this fix?

PANGLOSS

As for me, sir—I have spent my life maintaining that everything was going fine—When they stole, pillaged, murdered my fellow creatures in the name of principle or even in the name of nothing at all, when the Inquisitor wanted to hang me for teaching him to reason fairly, I declared that all was for the best in the best of all worlds. Here it's impossible for me to find that everything is for the best since no one steals here, murder is unknown, and there are no Inquisitors to burn or hang people. Funny country where one is so stupidly happy.

CANDIDE

It wouldn't be so stupid if Miss Cunegonde were here.

CACAMBO

Let's leave Miss Cunegonde where she is—You can be sure she's occupied—and do as she does. The women here are full of good will.

CANDIDE

Evidently it's not good will they lack.

CACAMBO

I would say even there there's too much of it. It's much too easy. Love without incident has the effect on me of a buffet lunch. I need complications rebuffs, jealousies, and knife cuts. Long Live European Love!

MARTIN

Long Live European Life Style! Ah—the arguments, the turning topsy-turvy—the brawls, the punches in the mouth and fist fights—the frightened bourgeois, beating up the police . Now that's the life, that is!

PANGLOSS

Ah, the beautiful discussions in the universities, courtrooms and congregations, the beautiful speeches that say nothing and the prepared beautiful phrases—That's the life.

CANDIDE

Ah—Cunegonde! That's the life.

CACAMBO

Ah! The women that you love and who deceive you—The ones you don't love and who stick to you like glue—Ah the beautiful nights under the stars where you sleep under bridges after having tightened your belt with courage, the races in pursuit of money which flees and the expedients, the stratagems, the ruses, the audacious strokes—That's the life.

MARTIN

Comrades, we're in agreement. Let's leave this shore when women are indolent and men are limp. Let's return to the old world where they dispute, where they grumble, where they insult, where they threaten, where they strike—Only there is it true—Only there is it good.

CACAMBO

But before all else, let's fill our wallets and pockets with gold nuggets, diamonds and stones. That will be useful to us—among the civilized to purchase consciences (Taking ample provisions of gold as Martin and

Pangloss imitate him) With this—we will be masters everywhere.

CANDIDE

Men are the same everywhere—for sale everywhere—

MARTIN

Everywhere—Only the money differs. Come—let's be on our way.

PANGLOSS

Where are we going?

MARTIN

There are only two cities in the world where one has money—Paris for parties—Venice for love.

CANDIDE

Ah, Venice, that's poetic! I wanted to have my honeymoon there with Cunegonde.

CACAMBO

I will go find her for you in Buenos Aires and I will escort her to you in Venice.

MARTIN

We will find you there after having been worn out by Paris.

PANGLOSS

I've heard it said they have the most beautiful theatres, the most brilliant universities and the deliberative assemblies are the most loquacious, all this is needed to descant, to discuss, dispute, comment, criticize and philosophize—So long live Paris! (As they are about to leave, their pockets filled with gold, a pure and moving song arises from the natives—celebrating nature, peace, liberty and Brotherhood. A bit impressed Martin and his companions stop and listen)

CANDIDE

(In ecstasy) How beautiful that is.

MARTIN

(With a sweeping gesture) Bullshit! (He starts to leave, his companions follow him with their heavy loads—Candide, the last, stops as if he can hardly tear himself away from the charm of this country—The curtain falls slowly while the glorious song unfolds its grand strophes)

CURTAIN

ACT IV
SCENE 7[1]

The action takes place in Paris in the salon of Mlle de Parolignac.

Very rich furniture—In the back—a card table.

AT RISE, gamblers fighting.

1st PLAYER

Why, sir you are cheating.

2nd PLAYER

Pardon, Excellency—it's you who are cheating—you have an extra card in your hand.

1st PLAYER

The Salon of La Parolignac is a dive! You meet the 40 thieves here.

---

1. This scene was omitted in performance.

2nd PLAYER

Thief yourself. (Noise of smacks. Pangloss who was sitting at a table and gambling rises and goes to wake up two sleeping lackeys striking them on the shoulder)

PANGLOSS

My friends—do your duty—(The lackeys beat the discontented gamblers off, not without tumult) It's unheard of. There's no way to work peacefully. The Parisians are becoming so susceptible—Evidently they've been rendered nervous by the Seven Years' War—(The Marquise enters) Ah! Here's our beautiful Marquise de Parolignac!

MARQUISE

(Bustling) Nothing new.

PANGLOSS

Deadly calm—except for the expulsions of two ruffians—(Aside) All is for the best in the best of demimondes.

MARQUISE

Heavy betting?

PANGLOSS

Yuck! Gamblers who hold on to their money and keep on the lookout. Luckily I am here—I watch the winning.

MARQUISE

We will have a lot of company tonight; I've issued many invitations (In a low voice). And that gentleman returned from the Indies whose pockets are full of gold, of pearls, of diamonds—We will see him soon?

PANGLOSS

He promised me to come.

MARQUISE

I am counting on you to teach him to play "Pharo."

PANGLOSS

You can count on it!

MARQUISE

Anyway, I intend that this soirée be most brilliant—The Marquise de Parolignac is receiving! They've spoken of us in the *Gazette de Holland*. (She turns toward the gamblers)

PANGLOSS

(Aside) Pangloss, my friend, here you are more philosopher than ever and that of the fine school of Plato, the Greek—(Moves off without leaving the stage)

1st PLAYER

(Approaching the Marquise) Marquise—they cheat here.

MARQUISE

Oh—so little—

2nd PLAYER (GAMBLER)

I admire the gentleman's talent. (Pointing to Pangloss) What do you call that swine?

MARQUISE

My friend, the Chevalier de Pangloss! Why, he's the most honest man in the world—I have high esteem for his person and his talents—You know I receive only men of wit—Console yourself for having lost some money at play—Anyway, tonight you will have compensation. Think that you are going to meet here all the finest in politics, literature, theatre, music, dance—We will have Voltaire and the philosopher from Geneva.

GAMBLER

Marquise—You love philosophers too much and you turn trumps too often.

MARQUISE

They can do it every time.

GAMBLER

Indeed, that's what disturbs me—then—know that Mr. de Sartines, the Lieutenant of Police is one of my friends and I propose to tell him that here—

MARQUISE

(Ironic) Right, you'll meet him here tonight—You see, everything works out marvelously—

GAMBLER

You tell me so much!

MARQUISE

Complain!—Here's Miss Flora from the illustrious theatre with her Tax Collector—And you will see many others. (The Marquise and the gambler continue to argue while Flora and her Famer General make their entry)

FAMER GENERAL

This Marquise is an adventuress and receives company of dubious repute.

FLORA

My darling, I came here to amuse myself. Don't trouble my pleasure with your moralizing—The Marquise is charming and her guests are gay—that's the main thing. (The Marquise returns and pulls Flora to a sofa)

MARQUISE

Good evening, my pretty! What a success you've had! They are talking only of you at court and in the city. But when will the theatre you've had your Famer General build for you open?

FLORA

It will be finished next month. A marvel! Red and blue—and garlands everywhere—Mr. Fragonard is finishing his panels and I'm awaiting the Beauvais tapestries.

MARQUISE

A woman like you must have her theatre.

FLORA

Also, I will have my artists, my musicians, my authors—Ah, my comrades at the illustrious Theatre are going to rage! They refused me the best roles—they treated me in a manner unworthy of me—Flora! Well I shall have my, revenge—All Paris is going to applaud Flora at Flora's.

PANGLOSS

(To Famer General) What, sir—you are complaining, you!

FAMER GENERAL

Chevalier, it's becoming impossible to live—So I've just expended 180,000 crowns on this theater for Miss Flora.

PANGLOSS

Not much for you! And Miss Flora is so pretty. (A pause) By the way do you know that the great scientist Vaucanson is in misery?

FAMER GENERAL

Bah! These scientists are Philosophers and content with little. He's not like Miss Flora—But who's that character in the turban?

PANGLOSS

The Prince of Transylvania—A habitué of the Salon of Madame de Parolignac—a charming man—who has no luck at play!

PRINCE OF TRANSYLVANIA

Indeed I play on bad luck—I've just lost 3,000 crowns and what with the change—11,000 piastres.

PANGLOSS

Would you like to try again, Milord?

PRINCE

That's all I ask.

PANGLOSS

That's easy—! Go play, Excellency—

PRINCE

Come—but the green tapestry never succeeds here except at the Peace Congress—(Going to sit down)

MARQUISE

(Interrupting) Gentlemen, I promised you some surprises for this evening. A little patience. (To

Pangloss) And that gentleman returning from the Indies? And our dancers? And our musicians?

PANGLOSS

They are coming.

MARQUISE

And your Philosophers?

PANGLOSS

They're not coming. But I have something to replace them with. Here's my friend Martin—he'll make a presentable Voltaire—I will play Jean-Jacques—Let's go prepare ourselves. (They leave)

MARQUISE

(To a newcomer) Ah—here's Miss de Beaumesnil. Good evening—my gorgeous one! (Sensational entry of Miss de Beaumesnil soon completely surrounded)

FLORA

(Jealous) Oh—They're thronging around that creature! Yuck!

FAMER GENERAL

She's an artist!

FLORA

An artist? That girl only comes on stage so as to show her legs!

PANGLOSS

They're pretty legs and they say the Prince de Conti much appreciates them—

FLORA

It's a shame! (Aglae approaches and Flora goes toward her) Good evening, my darling! How happy I am to see you! You know I applauded you so much yesterday evening at the Opera—you were adorable!

MISS DE BEAUMESNIL

You are too good—and I love you so much! By the way, I've got to tell you—I'm going to have my theatre—yes, the Prince de Conti—(She continues her tale dragging Flora off)

MARQUISE

(To a dramatic author) My dear author, when will you give us a beautiful tragedy?

AUTHOR

You can't be thinking of it? A tragedy!—A play of

ideas? Why the public no longer wants it. Alas! It prefers a spectacle to please its eyes and facilitate its digestion—to the most eloquent tirades—Ah, the water level has been low since the war! But I am working all the same. I am preparing a play that will please both Court and Town—

MARQUISE

I am sure of it! Tell us about this masterpiece in which your wit won't fail to sparkle.

AUTHOR

(Bitterly) Oh—for sure—it will be a sparkling play.

MARQUISE

Doubtless, you are putting it naked into the human heart?

AUTHOR

You will indeed see naked things. It will have 1,200 costumes of extraordinary richness and so light that the public will be able to see all the talents of those who wear them; forty scenes entirely new, lit by 10,000 candles—three hundred girls who are the most pretty in Paris—and who will be splendidly dressed in a pair of garters and a fan—

MARQUISE

It will be magnificent—And the subject of this play?

AUTHOR

I'm still looking for one—But the main thing is done—Since we have the scenes, the costumes and the scantily clad girls. And then, is a text really necessary? The public cares so little about it. As to that, it is delighted with the magic lantern. Like children, it prefers pictures to text. What's to be done? (Sensational entry of Cunegonde who's become an actress)

MARQUISE

The delicious Zenobia d'Endos—our great artist. (Murmurs of admiration)

AUTHOR

(To the Prince of Transylvania) She's the woman of the day. One hundred scandal mongers tell us without cease of her lovers, her dogs, her jewels, her lawsuit.

PRINCE

Ah! These Parisiennes!

AUTHOR

But she's not a Parisienne—What an idea! She comes

to us, they say, from America, like all the great stars and she's hardly disembarked a month. But already two madmen have killed themselves for her—eyes which are beautiful enough—and almost every day she loses a pearl necklace.

PRINCE

Present me, I entreat you—

PANGLOSS

(To Cunegonde) His Highness, the Prince of Transylvania—Miss Zenobia d'Endus—

CUNEGONDE

(Giving her hand for the prince to kiss)

Prince.

(Very dignified—presenting the old woman) My mother! (Kneeling bow to the Old Woman)

MARQUISE

When will you debut in the Italians, my gorgeous?

CUNEGONDE

I don't know anymore. I'm going to have my theatres. In one I will dance, in the other I will sing—In the third I will act comedy.

FLORA

These girls!

MISS DE BEAUMESNIL

One's not enough for these creatures.

AUTHOR

(To Prince) They all have their own theatres but as yet their mother's don't have box seats.

PRINCE

I intend to marry that one (To Old Woman) Good old dear, I shall marry your daughter!

OLD WOMAN

Oh, Prince! What an honor! (She whispers to Cunegonde who smiles, looking at the Prince. Pangloss returns in the costume of Jean-Jacques Rousseau, Martin as Voltaire—)

FLORA

Who's that Armenian? (The guests have recognized the new arrival and circle around them)

MARQUISE

A great Philosopher! (To Pangloss) What an honor to receive the author of *Divine du Village*.

PANGLOSS

(As Jean-Jacques) Don't mention that bagatelle. I am the author of the *Social Contract*. (He is surrounded, congratulated)

FLORA

I've read all your books! How well you speak of Nature—

CLARA

I've poured tears over the *New Héloïse*.

MISS DE BEAUMESNIL

You employ sublime accents when you speak of motherhood.

JEAN-JACQUES

Ladies, I am confused—You read me—that's very fine. But do you apply my theories? Are you leading the simple and natural existence that I have described? Do you have children?

ALL

(Laughing) No way! Children? What an idea!

AUTHOR

(Aside) As for him, he's got it—but no one knows what's become of them!

LACKEY

(Announcing) Monsieur Voltaire! (Enter Martin disguised as Voltaire. A new sensation)

JEAN-JACQUES

My dear colleague, I admire you, even though you've been very severe with my philosophy—

VOLTAIRE

What a joy to meet you and tell you how much I love and admire the author of the *Social Contract*—

JEAN-JACQUES

I was going to say as much of the immortal author of the Virgin (Martin installs himself in an armchair at the right, Pangloss in an armchair at the left)

PANGLOSS

I believe I've demonstrated in my works that war is a frightful evil that we must suppress.

MARTIN

Excellent idea! If only you could suppress earthquakes—

PANGLOSS

The last war must be the last war.

MARTIN

I ask nothing better but I am skeptical enough.

PANGLOSS

And why?

MARTIN

Because I have the honor to know King Frederick the Great, who writes bad French verse but drills excellent Prussian soldiers!

PANGLOSS

We will form a league of nations that won't fight—

MARTIN

That will be a league of sheep against wolves.

PANGLOSS

You make men worse than they are—I believe them good—in their essence.

MARTIN

Oh—it's not that they are very bad—But they are extremely stupid.

PANGLOSS

You slander them—I think, for my part, virtue and sensibility are spread everywhere but oppressed and constrained by civilization. We are headed for a society where love and justice will reign, benevolence and brotherhood.

MARTIN

(Scornfully) Benevolence, brotherhood. Illusions, my dear dreamer. Universal peace—a chimera! Observe that all our time is spent in quarrels—Jesuits against Jansenists; men of the Parliament against the Court, men of letters against men of letters; courtiers against courtiers, financiers against the people; wives against husbands—relatives against relatives—It's an eternal war—

PANGLOSS

You hate your fellow creatures?

MARTIN

I do some of them this honor. Others I scorn. I distrust the rest.

PANGLOSS

You must be really wretched?

MARTIN

Me?—I laugh ceaselessly.

PANGLOSS

(Rising) Your laughing does evil.

MARTIN

(Also rising) Perhaps less than your sensibility—(They move away arguing)

MARQUISE

(To the ladies) They've announced to me the gentleman returned from the Indies—Here he is! (Enter Candide magnificently dressed)

FLORA

Why he is charming!

MISS DE BEAUMESNIL

Don't they say he's returned from the Indies with his pockets full of diamonds? (They surround Candide except Cunegonde who is seated at a gaming table all by herself)

MARQUISE

Dear friend! How I share in your happiness—You are at home here—your face, your misfortunes make you sympathetic to all.

CANDIDE

Alas, my misfortunes are not over!

MARQUISE

What can I do to console you?

AGLAE and FLORA

What can we do? Speak.

CANDIDE

Return Cunegonde to me.

ALL

Cunegonde.

CUNEGONDE

(Recognizing Candide) Candide, my darling Candide.

OLD WOMAN

Hush! The Prince is there—

CANDIDE

Yes, the most noble, the most wise, the most beautiful of women. For her I've been whipped and whipped again—I was almost burned alive—I've suffered a thousand ills—and I love her more than ever—and her absence causes my despair—I've even composed a love song about her—very touching and very poetic and I ask your permission to sing it to you. It does me so much good to speak of her even in music (Meanwhile Cunegonde has turned giving signs of surprise then of increasing emotion)

MARQUISE

Why then you will be ravished—won't you ladies—right gentlemen? (All the guests agree with polite eagerness)

CANDIDE

It's called "I lost my Cunegonde." (At these words Cunegonde rises and approaches Candide from the rear. He sings accompanied by the Marquise at the harpsichord)

(Singing) Tell me—do you know her?
Of the girls from Westphalia
Cunegonde is the prettiest
Tell me do you know her?
She is the blondest of the blondes
And whoever sees her is smitten
Ah, for me there's nothing more valuable
For I've lost my Cunegonde!
There's no more happiness for me
And I don't cling to life
Since she's been ravished from me
There's no more happiness for me!
Without respite, through the vast world
I've searched for her—but in vain
Ah! Show me the right road
For I've lost my Cunegonde.
Cunegonde was my only treasure
Without her everything to me seems empty
Pity the unfortunate Candide
Cunegonde was his only treasure
Also, I say all around
If I must no longer see her allures
I aspire to die ASAP
For I've lost my Cunegonde

But why suspect love
No, I want to believe in her still
Love will return the one I love
But why suspect love
One day on the earth or on the ocean
The Gods, become less cruel
Will in the end fulfill my wishes,
And give me back my Cunegonde!

(After the song, exclamations: "He's charming—Delicious! Poetic! Touching!")

MARQUISE

Where is she—this young Miss Cunegonde?

CANDIDE

I don't know—and I will give everything I have to meet her again. (At this moment Cunegonde takes a step she is ravished and hides behind a group)

MARQUISE

(To Candide) Your sensibility does your honor—But for this evening drive your cares away. Come play at Pharo! Unlucky in love, lucky at cards (Sighing, Candide goes to gamble. He pulls from his pocket fistfuls of gold. One can hear shouts of admiration)

CUNEGONDE

(Who has listened to Candide with emotion) Let me alone, I want to speak to him.

OLD WOMAN

Watch out! That young man is the cause of all your misfortunes and it's not at the moment of becoming a Princess that he ought to compromise your situation (Enter a Negro orchestra led by Cacambo)

MARQUISE

Ah—These are our musicians.

CANDIDE

Cacambo? You, here! And Miss Cunegonde?

CACAMBO

I've followed her trail—She's here—you will see her.

CANDIDE

Heavens!

CACAMBO

I will tell you this—I am delayed—I must play two pieces here—I am coming from the Duchess of

Montauban, where I played three—When I leave, I am running to the Duke of Miralda's to whom I will grant—one—I don't know where to rush to next—

CANDIDE

You've become a virtuoso?

CACAMBO

Not at all! I don't know a note of music. No more do my artists. But they find we have more talent than the musicians of the Opera. We pound very hard no matter how, no matter on what—

MARQUISE

(To Cacambo) Maestro our guests are getting impatient.

CACAMBO

Marquise—we are at your command. (Black music—Much emotion amongst the guests. Exclamations "Oh, charming! Ravishing, Exquisite—Adorable!")

MARQUISE

(After the first piece) Delicious! And such feeling! But we must dance! Play that new dance for us that all Paris is doting on. (The guests dance a dance with modern steps and eighteenth-century bows and scrapes)

POLICE OFFICER

On behalf of the King! (All stop) I am desolate, but I have to assure myself of all persons present.

MR. DE SARTINES

(To the officer) Sir, I congratulate—You've come at the right moment. But I'm sure you have no business with me?

OFFICER

Milord!

(Bowing—Mr. de Sartines leaves. Other guests are able to escape.)

PRINCE OF TRANSYLVANIS

Diplomatic corps.

OFFICER

Excellence, you are free! (The Ambassador withdraws)

FAMER GENERAL

Famer General, friend of the Superintendent.

OFFICER

(Bowing) Pass, sir. (The same routine for the following characters)

FLORA

(Very dignified) Miss Flora of the Theatre Flora.

OFFICER

(Bowing deeply) Miss—(She leaves)

MISS DE BEAUMESNIL

Miss de Beaumesnil—of the Opera, friend of Prince Conti.

OFFICER

(Bending double) Miss! (She leaves)

AUTHOR

Author of the *Clumsy Husband*—and friend of Miss Flora.

OFFICER

(Respectfully) Pass, sir. (The author leaves)

MARTIN

(Proudly) Author of *Merope*!

OFFICER

Pass.

PANGLOSS

(With false humility) Citizen of Geneva.

OFFICER

(Turning his back) So be it—be off as well. (Pangloss leaves; Cunegonde is haughtily seated)

That's always the way it is—The biggest fish pass through the net.

CANDIDE

Robbed, I've been robbed. They've taken everything from me (He turns out his pockets—At these words Cunegonde with a gesture of scorn gets ready to leave)

OFFICER

(Aside) This one will pay for the others. (Aloud) Sir, I arrest you in the name of the King.

CANDIDE

Me? What have I done? I am a victim! I've been robbed, made a fool of, tricked.

OFFICER

They all say that! Come, friend, follow me. (The soldiers grab Candide)

CANDIDE

(Noticing Cunegonde) Heavens!—You! It's you! You here—oh joy! (He escapes from the officers and rushes towards Cunegonde who recoils, disdainfully)

CUNEGONDE

I don't know you, sir.

CANDIDE

Aren't you Miss Cunegonde?

CUNEGONDE

I am Miss Zenobia of the Zenobia Theatre.

OFFICER

(Bowing) Pass, Madame.

CUNEGONDE

(Leaves with dignity) Penniless!

OFFICER

(To two soldiers) Grab that insolent fellow for me. (The soldiers grab Candide and lead him brutally. One of the soldiers kicks him in the ass)

CANDIDE

(Protecting his ass) Again!

CURTAIN

ACT V
SCENE 8

The Inn in Venice. The stage represents a dining room in Venetian style. A huge table lit by candles.

AT RISE, the servant is busy lighting the last candles.

CANDIDE

We are here at last—in Venice!

MARTIN

We are here at last in a dining room. I've got a huge appetite, I admit it.

PANGLOSS

How everything works out, gentlemen. Our friend Candide is going to see his darling Cunegonde and we are going to sup.

SERVANT

Your Excellencies desire supper?

MARTIN

Our Excellencies desire it passionately!

SERVANT

You will be served in a few minutes, I am going to give orders to the kitchen. (He leaves)

MARTIN

So long as the supper is good!

CANDIDE

No, so long as I see Cunegonde again—For it's for her that I came to Venice. And after how many disappointments. Happily I still have a few diamonds.

MARTIN

So long as diamond remain, all goes well—we have men and women—Without diamonds nobody.

CANDIDE

You are severe!

MARTIN

That's because I've lived.

CANDIDE

I prefer Pangloss' philosophy to yours. Pangloss is a much greater Philosopher than you—for he consoles me and he promises me what I desire—That is to say Cunegonde's love (To Pangloss) Right, Pangloss—I am going to see her again.

PANGLOSS

You love her—she loves you and Venice is the city of love—

CANDIDE

Yes, but still—Cacambo must keep his promise—And I am worried.

PANGLOSS

Confidence! The effects and their causes—You will see Cacambo again (Enter Cacambo) You see?

CANDIDE

Cacambo! O joy! (Embracing him) Cunegonde is here without a doubt? Where is she? Lead me to her so I can die of joy with her.

CACAMBO

Cunegonde is not here—she is living with the Prince

of Transylvania on the shores of the Propontis.

CANDIDE

Ah! Heavens! But were she in China I would fly there—Let's leave.

CACAMBO

We will leave after supper.

CANDIDE

No—Right away.

MARTIN and PANGLOSS

(Forcefully) Ah! No—We are supping first. (Candide desolated goes to sit in a corner)

PANGLOSS

(To Cacambo) Between ourselves, I wasn't hoping to see you here again.

CACAMBO

Sir, I haven't had any luck—I will tell you this From one adventure to another—I have become stranded in Venice where I am a slave.

PANGLOSS

Slave.

CACAMBO

Yes—I cannot tell you more—Here's my master. (They enter one by one Indian file gravely, a little like automatons while the orchestra plays variations of Carnival at Venice. Behind them the servants bring plates. The four Kings sit at the same time, unfolding their napkins at the same time making exactly the same gestures and without looking at each other and without paying any attention to what they may be doing—Pangloss, vaguely uneasy takes a place at the table and by gestures urges Candide to do so as well. Candide obeys but halfheartedly. The four Monarchs eat with automatic gestures. Candide, Pangloss and Martin, learning from their example end by doing so as well. Rhythmic music. Silence of the guests.)

CACAMBO

(Leaning towards the napkin of his master) Sire, Your Majesty will leave when he chooses—The vessel is ready—! (Cacambo leaves. The meal continues. The servant serves wine and dishes)

SERVANT

(Leaning towards another Monarch) Sire, Your

Majesty's chair is prepared and the boat is ready. (The meal continues. The servant leans toward another Monarch) Sire I've prepared everything as ordered by Your Majesty. (The meal continues. The servant leans toward the 4th Monarch) Sire, Your Majesty will leave whenever you choose. (The meal continues. The Monarchs reply to the servant only by signs of their heads. Pangloss and Martin witness this with growing stupefaction. The servant leaves. Profound silence)

CANDIDE

Gentlemen, this is a singular joke. Why are you all Kings? As for me, I confess to you, that neither I, nor Pangloss, nor Martin are

PANGLOSS

And I am sufficiently drunk to believe this is a question of a carnival farce.

1st MONARCH

I am not joking and I don't give myself to any farce. I reign over Turkey—I've been the Grand Sultan for several years—They called me "The sick man" now I am "The dead man" I dethroned my brother—my nephew dethroned me—They cut the throats of my viziers—I am ending my life in the old harem; my nephew the Sultan allows me to travel sometimes for my health—and I come to spend the Carnival in

Venice.

2nd MONARCH

As for me, I pass for the most diplomatic of all Monarchs—for many years I only obtained success. From a little Prince I grew to be King, and then I made myself Tsar. Everything smiled on me. I was going to take Constantinople back from the infidels. Alas, taken with vertigo I declared war and placed myself on the wrong side. Victory betrayed me, I had to flee my capital. Ever since, I've known the bitterness of exile. I travel to console myself and I came to spend Carnival in Venice.

3rd MONARCH

As for me, I ruled over twenty nations and our Saint Peter, the Pope blessed me every day—But in mounting the throne I found war in my realm, famine and despair. My predecessor, he too, was on the wrong side. My armies took flight, my people revolted. After a few months of ruling I was dethroned and obliged to leave my capital—Ever since I go from asylum to asylum—And I've come to spend Carnival at Venice.

4th MONARCH

As for me, I am— (Stops, then whispers a name)

ALL

What? It's you.

4th MONARCH

Yes, I know—I've aged—I let my beard grow and no one recognizes me, in this lamentable wreck the powerful Emperor of times gone by. (Silence, then continuing) They let me travel sometimes. Indeed, this city has seen me in times when I reigned. Dressed in white—helmeted in gold, I passed by standing in a golden gondola, before that palace where the beautiful guests of the Doge acclaimed me. Distant memories—And I came to spend the Carnival in Venice.

2nd MONARCH

If we are here—it's your fault.

3rd MONARCH

Assuredly, you dragged us all into this stupid war!

4th MONARCH

(Harshly) If you had done your duty you wouldn't be here.—Nor I for that matter. You abandoned me, betrayed me.

2nd MONARCH

Ah—indeed, for heaven's sake—you don't lack chutzpah.

3rd MONARCH

You are cynical.

4th MONARCH

What! You dare to speak to me in that tone! To me?

1st MONARCH

(Very calm) My dear colleagues, what's the use of these quarrels? Your situation won't improve and perhaps even will get a bit worse. Say quite simply as I do, it was written! And let's be gay—for we came to spend the Carnival in Venice. (They become silent, motionless lugubrious. Cacambo half opens the door and makes a sign to his thee friends who rise, bow to the Monarchs and leave. The curtain falls slowly while the Monarchs remain fired in the immobility of statues.)

CURTAIN

ACT V
SCENE 9

Candide's Garden: a small kitchen garden with all sorts of vegetables shooting up. To the left a modest farm, to the right a gate cut by entry door. In front of the entry door—a large shaded road—In the back—the Bosphorus—the Golden Horn and in the distance—Constantinople.

Cacambo is gardening. Martin and Pangloss are seated. Candide is walking with a pensive air.

PANGLOSS

It seems that after so many storms, this little farm on the coast of the Bosphorus must be the harbor where we shall experience rest. Candide and Cunegonde are worried—Cacambo is working and we are reasoning—And so everything continues to head for the best in the best of worlds.

MARTIN

Everything, in sum, would go less badly if we didn't

have this slut of a Cunegonde whose physical aspect is offensive to our eyes and whose screechy voice galls our ears. Between ourselves, Candide was wrong to go find her at the Prince of Transylvania's where she was washing linen.

PANGLOSS

That Cunegonde was once the most beautiful Baroness in Westphalia—Her figure was divine, her face charming—her bearing majestic and her voice melodious.

MARTIN

She's changed a lot! All! Here she is. Save yourself if you can! (Martin goes to the side, Pangloss rises precipitously and moves to the other side. Cunegonde enters visibly very irritated. She is very disfigured, eyes bloodshot, throat depressed, cheeks shriveled, arms reddened. She rushes on Candide who tries to flee but too late)

CUNEGONDE

Ah, indeed—is this life here ever going to finish? Do you think I am pleased here, to live with chickens, rabbits and pigs—me—a Baroness with seventy-two quarters of nobility, daughter of one of the most powerful lords of Westphalia—and made to reign in courts?

OLD WOMAN

(Entering behind Cunegonde) What would I say, me—daughter of a Princess and a Pope, reduced to the miserable condition of a farm girl? It's a shame sir, to make a Princess Palestrini- Palestrina into a servant!

CANDIDE

But you aren't serving anyone here, from morning until night you don't lift a finger.

OLD WOMAN

And it's still more sad, sir—boredom devours me!

CUNEGONDE

As for me, I'm becoming neurasthenic. I want to return to my father's castle—to receive, give balls—hold courts of love—as is suitable to a person of my rank and my beauty. (Martin and Pangloss at a safe distance guffaw)

CANDIDE

Hold courts of love! But my poor friend, look at yourself in a mirror! Your face would put the most determined satyr to flight.

CUNEGONDE

That's too much! That's the way you insult beauty now.

OLD WOMAN

(Very threatening and attacking Candide from the other side) Yes, sir, you will confess that we are beautiful or we will scratch your eyes out. (Candide terrified recoils precipitously)

MARTIN

It's better to hear than be deaf.

PANGLOSS

Illusion is one of the great consolations granted to human creatures in misfortune.

OLD WOMAN

(To Martin and Pangloss) And you, too, impolite fellows, bad jokers, gross characters, we'll scratch them out—your eyes, if you don't confess and proclaim our beauty!

CUNEGONDE

(To Candide) As for you, sir, I call upon you to have me taken by carriage to the Castle of Thunder-ten-Tronchk, the castle of my fathers and the most beautiful of castles.

CANDIDE

My dear Cunegonde, I bought this farm with the gold remaining from Eldorado—that was left me by the Jews, the Greeks, the merchants and the functionaries. You have to adjust yourself. The castle of your father which (between ourselves) was infinitely less comfortable than this dwelling—the castle of your fathers no longer exists. You were violated by Bulgars, a Jew, an Inquisitor, a Hidalgo—you were a slave and washing linen on the shores of the Propontis when I purchased you back and married you.

CUNEGONDE

You married me! Why it's I, sir, who did you great honor, because I have seventy-two quarters of nobility well counted and authenticated whereas you have only seventy-one—seventy-one and a half not more.

CANDIDE

That's possible—but at the price butter is at, your quarters of nobility don't weigh heavily. Try to coin yours, you will see if you extract enough to buy a bushel of dried peas.

CUNEGONDE

You are a materiel being.

CANDIDE

I am a man of good sense, who having lived a lot in a few years I am beginning to understand life. Believe me, my poor, mad, woman—don't complain of a good bargain and continue to live here where you have your pot boiling in security—Thanks to that excellent Cacambo who works in the flower beds and goes to sell the vegetables in the market.

CACAMBO

(Who has interrupted his work to drink from his gourd, approaching) And even I begin to have my full of toiling like a good bugger—When these gentlemen-ladies pass their days making speeches!

CANDIDE

You hear him! If inaction weighs on you, if boredom gnaws you do as he does—work!

CUNEGONDE

Work, me! The daughter of Baron Thunder-ten-Tronchk—! You insult me, sir I prefer to be bored—

CANDIDE

At your ease!

OLD WOMAN

In short, I want to know which is the worst—to experience all the miseries through which we've all past or rather to remain here and do nothing?

CANDIDE

That's a great question?

MARTIN

Man is born to live in convulsions of uncertainty or in the lethargy of boredom—Take the question—turn it on every side—I defy you to reach any other conclusion.

PANGLOSS

Pardon, my dear chap, and I pretend to sustain, by supporting myself with healthy philosophy—that boredom and unrest are necessary to the happiness of mankind and that universal reason—

CUNEGONDE

(Beside herself) The universal reason again! Words again! Phrases, speeches! Enough, enough, enough, you are only chatterers and good for nothing!

PANGLOSS

(With dignity)

We are Philosophers—

CUNEGONDE

That's just what I meant. (To Candide) And you, sir, who shelter and sustain these parasites—you are only a dastard, a blunderer and a serf.

CANDIDE

You say?

CUNEGONDE

Yes, a serf that I will have whipped by my servants when my beautiful castle of Thunder-ten-Tronchk has been returned to me. Serf! Serf! Serf!

CANDIDE

(Slapping her at random) There! Take that with you to your beautiful castle. (Cunegonde lets out inarticulate screams—The old woman receives her in her arms. A good old Turk stops on the road with baskets of fruit and confectionaries. He comes in pushing his carriage and waving his bell)

GOOD OLD TURK

Bananas, pistachios, ground nuts—beautiful Valensians. These are the fruits of my garden—confectionaries prepared by the white hands of my daughters, who also make perfumes, at your service ladies and gentlemen. Here's extract of rose, of bergamot tree of amber, and essences, that in all department stores you would wish for—Syrians at the price of a 100 pastries—They are prepared in my kitchen and I sell them by weight, five piastres per pound—and you can't get better.

CANDIDE

You are an honest merchant.

MARTIN

Are there any?

GOOD OLD TURK

There's me.

PANGLOSS

This man proves by his example the excellence of human nature. All is for the best in the best of worlds—since we find here Patriarchs and Philanthropists like you.

GOOD OLD TURK

I don't have any pretentions I am simply a good old Turk—the good old Turk of days gone by whose naval officers traveled in the Orient and were spoken of in their novels.

MARTIN

Really, this good old Turk here is not an imaginary person—? He exists?

GOOD OLD TURK

As you see. I have twenty acres of land I cultivate it with my children. When I've finished cultivating it, I make children. I have seventy-seven children with fourteen different wives—So I join usefulness to pleasantness and I distract myself in my family—Work and family keep three great evils away—from us—boredom, vice and need. Always at your service, and thank you kindly ladies and gentlemen.

CANDIDE

(Shocked) Fourteen wives!

GOOD OLD TURK

Exactly and here's the fourteenth (Deep curtsy by the fourteenth wife of the good old Turk)

CUNEGONDE

(Thoughtful) Seventy-seven children.

14th WIFE

Permit me to present them to you (She makes a sign) Psst! (Seventy-seven children file by in silhouette)

CUNEGONDE

(Caressing the children) How sweet they are! They are completely cute.

CANDIDE

And fourteen wives. Does that work?

GOOD OLD TURK

With a whip!

PANGLOSS

That's the good way! (The good old Turk moves away with his wife and his seventy-seven children—Cries of "fruit, citrus, sorbets—bananas, pistachios, nuts.")

CANDIDE

That good old man is a sage and he seems to me to be of a type much preferable to those monarchs we supped with in Venice. Wisdom is to cultivate our garden. It's time the little peas ask to drink—Let's be good to the little peas.

MARTIN

To work without reasoning is the only way to support this bitch of a life.

CUNEGONDE

Let's go—I am going to make my cakes.

OLD WOMAN

I am going to look to the linen.

CANDIDE

As for me, I've become misanthropic I will busy myself with the animals.

PANGLOSS

As for me, I remain a Philosopher—one is needed in all organized society—I will comment on the benefits of universal reason and I will prove that all is for the best in the best of all possible worlds—For if you hadn't been kicked out of a beautiful castle with big kicks in the ass—if you hadn't been imprisoned and beaten by the Bulgarians, whipped by the Inquisitor, robbed by the Jews and the merchants, and mistreated by all those with whom you had business—you wouldn't be here eating citrus, confectionaries and pistachios.

CANDIDE

That's well said, but we must cultivate our garden.

PANGLOSS

Cultivate our garden!

CANDID, MARTIN, CACAMBO

Let's cultivate our garden! (They pass by—one bringing a shovel the other a watering pot and the third a wheelbarrow—)

CURTAIN

ABOUT THE AUTHOR

Frank J. Morlock has written and translated many plays since retiring from the legal profession in 1992. His translations have also appeared on Project Gutenberg, the Alexandre Dumas Père web page, Literature in the Age of Napoléon, Infinite Artistries.com, and Munsey's (formerly Blackmask). In 2006 he received an award from the North American Jules Verne Society for his translations of Verne's plays. He lives and works in México.

www.ingramcontent.com/pod-product-compliance
Lightning Source LLC
LaVergne TN
LVHW041621070426
835507LV00008B/370